HOW SWEET (AND SAVORY) IT IS!
DISCOVER ALL THE FLAVORS YOU'VE BEEN MISSING
IN
CORINNE T. NETZER'S
101 LOW SODIUM RECIPES

FOLLOWING DOCTOR'S ORDERS DOES NOT HAVE TO LEAVE
YOU OR YOUR FAMILY FEELING DEPRIVED AT MEALTIMES.
COOKING WITH CORINNE T. NETZER CHASES AWAY THE
LOW SODIUM-DIET BLUES WITH VIBRANT, FULL-FLAVORED
DISHES SO GOOD THEY BRING BACK THE PLEASURE YOU'VE
BEEN MISSING.
IMAGINE THE SMILES WHEN YOU SERVE:

The Appetizer
♦ Shrimp-Stuffed Cherry Tomatoes

The Soup
♦ Spinach and Kale Soup with Wild Rice

The Salad
♦ Vegetable Platter with Four Fabulous Dips

The Entree
♦ Cornish Hens on a Bed of Artichoke Hearts

The Side Dishes
♦ Green Rice, Red Cabbage, and
Apple Slaw with Poppy-Seed Dressing

The Dessert
♦ Plum and Almond Crepes

SURPRISINGLY LOW CALORIE—VERY LOW SODIUM
UNCOMPROMISINGLY GOOD!

▶ ▶ ▶ ▶ ▶ ▶ ▶

101 LOW SODIUM RECIPES

◆ ◆ ◆ ◆ ◆

QUANTITY SALES

Most Dell books are available at special quantity discounts when purchased in bulk by corporations, organizations, or groups. Special imprints, messages, and excerpts can be produced to meet your needs. For more information, write to: Dell Publishing, 666 Fifth Avenue, New York, NY 10103. Attention: Director, Diversified Sales.

Please specify how you intend to use the books (e.g., promotion, resale, etc.).

INDIVIDUAL SALES

Are there any Dell books you want but cannot find in your local stores? If so, you can order them directly from us. You can get any Dell book currently in print. For a complete up-to-date listing of our books and information on how to order, write to: Dell Readers Service, Box DR, 666 Fifth Avenue, New York, NY 10103.

THE
CORINNE T. NETZER
GOOD EATING SERIES

▶▶▶▶▶▶▶▶▶▶

101 LOW SODIUM RECIPES

◆ ◆ ◆ ◆ ◆

Corinne T. Netzer

A Dell Trade Paperback

A DELL TRADE PAPERBACK

Published by
Dell Publishing
a division of
Bantam Doubleday Dell Publishing Group, Inc.
666 Fifth Avenue
New York, New York 10103

Designed by Rhea Braunstein

Illustrated by Alice Sorensen

*Cover photo: Corn and Pepper
Chowder, p.45*

ISBN: 0-440-50419-8

Printed in the United States of America
Published simultaneously in Canada
April 1993
10   9   8   7   6   5   4   3   2   1
HCR

CONTENTS

INTRODUCTION

When I was growing up, the only guidance I received concerning sodium was "don't salt it until you taste it." Of course, we now know that this directive didn't go nearly far enough.

Of all the studies regarding nutrition and health undertaken in recent years, those on sodium have perhaps emerged as the most controversial. Studies have shown that the average American diet contains far more sodium than is necessary for good health. And as more and more foods are analyzed, we have come to learn that sodium is naturally present in all foods to varying degrees.

Unfortunately, salt is an acquired taste and we've become used to sprucing up our meals with a sprinkle here and there. Although I have found that the taste for salt eventually decreases, simply eliminating the problem ingredient often leaves us with food that is bland and unappealing: in other words, not Good Eating.

In *101 Low Sodium Recipes* you will find recipes that are not only healthful but flavorful—recipes that will enable you to stay on a low sodium diet without sacrificing good taste.

Each recipe includes a sodium count per portion. These figures are based on the latest nutritional data obtained from the United States Department of Agriculture and various food producers and processors.

While this book features low sodium recipes, overall health considerations have been taken into account as well.

Enjoy!

C.T.N.

STOCKS, SAUCES, and DRESSINGS

♦ ♦ ♦ ♦ ♦

LOW SODIUM CHICKEN STOCK

▶ ▶

I can't think of a more useful item in my cooking reper-toire than homemade, low sodium, defatted stock. I like to have it available for cooking at all times. I keep one-cup containers in my freezer; I also freeze some in an ice cube tray, then release the stock cubes and store them in zip-tight plastic bags. I often add a cube to a touch of heated olive oil for steam-sautéeing onions, garlic, or vegetables in a covered saucepan.

Perhaps the most versatile of my stocks is this one, which is *always* on hand. In addition to using it as a cook-ing ingredient, I frequently heat up a mugful, with a few noodles thrown in, for a tasty and comforting treat on chilly days.

1¹/₂	pounds chicken parts
3	quarts water
1	cup dry white table wine
2	medium onions, chopped
2	large stalks celery with tops, chopped
2	large carrots, chopped
6	sprigs fresh parsley
1	bay leaf
1	clove garlic, peeled and quartered
1	teaspoon dried thyme
1	teaspoon dried tarragon
8	whole peppercorns or ¹/₂ teaspoon ground pepper

1. Place all ingredients in a large stockpot and bring to a boil. Cover, reduce heat, and simmer gently for 2 hours, stirring occasionally and adding more water if too much liquid evaporates. Remove from heat and cool slightly.

2. Pour stock through a fine strainer, or sieve lined with cheesecloth, into a large bowl. Using the back of a large spoon, press lightly on solids to extract liquid. Discard solids or reserve for another purpose and cool stock to room temperature.

3. Cover and refrigerate stock for several hours or until fat congeals on the surface. Skim off and discard fat. Stock is ready to use or can be frozen in serving-size containers.

MAKES ABOUT 2 QUARTS
APPROXIMATELY 25 MILLIGRAMS SODIUM PER CUP

◆ ◆ ◆ ◆ ◆

LOW SODIUM BEEF STOCK

▶ ▶

As with my chicken stock, my favorite beef stock is low in sodium, calories, and fat and may be used in many recipes featured in all five books of my Good Eating Series. Use it in stews, roasts, and soups or as the cooking liquid for rice and other grains, legumes, and vegetables.

1½ pounds beef marrow bones
½ pound lean chuck, cut into ½-inch cubes
3 quarts water
1 cup dry red table wine
2 large onions, diced
2 large stalks celery with tops, chopped
2 large carrots, chopped
6 sprigs fresh parsley
1 bay leaf
1 clove garlic, peeled and quartered
1 teaspoon dried thyme
1 teaspoon dried marjoram
8 whole peppercorns or ½ teaspoon freshly ground pepper

1. Place all ingredients in a large stockpot and bring to a boil. Cover, reduce heat to low, and simmer gently for 2 hours, stirring occasionally and adding more water if too much liquid evaporates. Remove from heat and cool slightly.

2. Pour stock through a fine strainer or sieve lined with cheesecloth into a large bowl. Remove bones, then press

lightly on remaining solids to extract as much liquid as possible. Discard solids or reserve for another purpose and cool stock to room temperature.

3. Cover stock and refrigerate for several hours or until fat congeals on the surface. Skim off and discard fat. Stock is ready to use or can be frozen in serving-size containers.

MAKES ABOUT 2 QUARTS
APPROXIMATELY 25 MILLIGRAMS SODIUM PER CUP

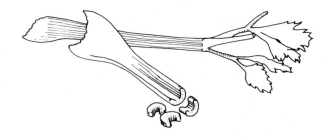

LOW SODIUM VEGETABLE STOCK

I am among those "waste not, want not" folks who enjoy eating leftover vegetables. After carefully removing the bay leaf, cloves, and peppercorns, I blend the vegetables to a chunky consistency in the food processor and eat them as a porridge or freeze the puree for later use as a thickening agent for vegetable soups, pasta sauces, and stews.

10	cups water
1	cup dry red or white table wine
1	large onion, chopped
4	cloves garlic, peeled and left whole
2	stalks celery with leaves, quartered
2	carrots, quartered
2	leeks, white and tender greens, well rinsed and chopped
1	medium tomato, chopped
1	parsnip, halved
6	sprigs fresh parsley
1	bay leaf
2	whole cloves
6	whole peppercorns

1. Combine all ingredients in a large stockpot and bring to a boil. Reduce heat and simmer, partially covered, for 1 hour, stirring occasionally and adding more water if too much liquid evaporates. Remove from heat and cool slightly.

2. Pour stock through a fine strainer, or sieve lined with

cheesecloth, into a large bowl. Using the back of a large spoon, press lightly on remaining solids to extract as much liquid as possible. Discard solids or reserve for another purpose and cool liquid to room temperature. Stock is ready to use or can be frozen in serving-size containers.

MAKES ABOUT 2 QUARTS
APPROXIMATELY 15 MILLIGRAMS SODIUM PER CUP

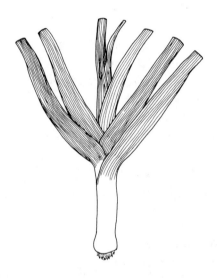

ALL-PURPOSE TOMATO SAUCE

The sauces created by the chef often make or break the reputation of a restaurant, and can turn a simple dish into party fare. This is such a sauce.

My All-Purpose Tomato Sauce is wonderful in stews or over pasta, broiled meats, poultry, or fish. Feel free to improvise—add sun-dried tomatoes or a dash of balsamic vinegar, use shallots instead of onion, substitute fresh basil for the oregano, and spread the sauce on sliced crusty bread. The possibilities are as varied as your imagination.

2	teaspoons olive oil
1	large onion, diced
1	clove garlic, minced
4	cups chopped fresh ripe tomatoes
2	tablespoons no-salt-added tomato paste
3/4	cup water
2	tablespoons chopped fresh parsley or 1 tablespoon dried
1	tablespoon chopped fresh oregano or 1 teaspoon dried
1	teaspoon dried basil
	Freshly ground pepper to taste

1. Heat oil in a large nonstick skillet. Add onion and garlic and cook over medium heat, stirring often, until onion is translucent.

2. Add remaining ingredients and continue stirring over medium heat for 5 minutes. Cover, reduce heat to low, and simmer gently, stirring occasionally, for 30 minutes.

3. Remove cover, raise heat to medium, and cook for about 5 minutes or until sauce thickens and liquid is slightly reduced.

MAKES ABOUT 3 CUPS
APPROXIMATELY 15 MILLIGRAMS SODIUM PER ½ CUP

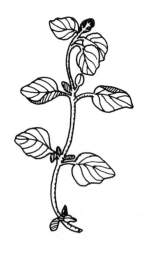

◆ ◆ ◆ ◆ ◆

SPICY TOMATO SAUCE

▶▶▶▶▶▶▶▶▶▶▶▶▶▶▶▶▶▶▶▶▶

This sauce has some bite, making it very different in character and flavor from my All-Purpose Tomato Sauce (page 9). You can make it as hot or as mild as you like by adjusting the quantity of hot pepper sauce or flakes.

Good over pasta, cooked with shellfish, in soups, on ground meat and poultry patties, on pizza, or on toasted pita wedges topped with low sodium cottage or ricotta cheese for a tangy pita pizza.

2	teaspoons olive oil
1	large onion, diced
2	cloves garlic, minced
6	ripe plum tomatoes, chopped
3	tablespoons no-salt-added tomato paste
$^1/_2$	cup dry red table wine
$^1/_2$	teaspoon sugar
1	teaspoon Worcestershire sauce
2	tablespoons minced fresh basil or 1 tablespoon dried
1	tablespoon minced fresh parsley
2	teaspoons dried oregano
1	teaspoon dried thyme
	Freshly ground pepper to taste
	Dash hot pepper sauce or $^1/_4$ teaspoon hot red pepper flakes, or to taste

1. Heat oil in a large nonstick skillet. Add onion and garlic and cook, stirring often, until onion is translucent.

2. Add remaining ingredients and stir over medium heat until blended. Cover, reduce heat to low, and simmer gently, stirring occasionally, for 30 minutes.

3. Raise heat to medium, remove cover, and cook for about 5 minutes or until sauce thickens and liquid is slightly reduced.

MAKES ABOUT 3 CUPS

APPROXIMATELY 27 MILLIGRAMS SODIUM PER ½ CUP

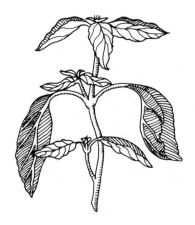

CREAMY CURRY SAUCE

Curry, a blend of three to fifty(!) different spices, is available mild, mildly hot, hot, and very hot. Other than that, one sniff will tell you how individual brands differ. Imagine how varied the curry powders are in India where they are prepared from whole spices ground or pounded daily. There they are mixed according to ancient recipes handed down from generation to generation, their secrets guarded as carefully as the original formula for *Coca-Cola*!

Unless you are one of the growing "must-be-from-scratch" curry fanciers, the use of commercial curry powders is perfectly legitimate. If you do choose to mix your own, you can follow my recommendations or you can amplify the flavor with extra spices (additional cayenne will make it as hot as you wish), fruit rinds, garlic, ginger root, and fresh herbs such as rosemary, parsley, dill, anise, and/or thyme. Just a word of caution: each amplification of flavor should be strongly considered and any wild inspiration to toss every spice on the shelf into the pot strongly resisted. Add spices a little at a time, and taste as you go along.

Use this sauce to enhance anything—vegetables, legumes, rice, noodles, meats, fish, poultry—with the possible exception of dessert.

2 teaspoons vegetable oil
1 clove garlic, minced
1/2 medium onion, minced
1 tablespoon fresh lemon juice

2   teaspoons minced fresh parsley
2   tablespoons curry powder or 1 teaspoon each:
    ground ginger, cumin, cardamom, coriander,
    and turmeric
2   cups Low Sodium Chicken Stock (page 3)
    Freshly ground pepper to taste
1/4   teaspoon cayenne, or to taste
1   tablespoon cornstarch
3/4   cup low fat plain yogurt

1. Heat oil in a large nonstick saucepan. Add garlic and onion and stir over medium heat until onion is translucent. Drizzle lemon juice over onions, then sprinkle with parsley and curry powder or combination of spices. Stir to blend.

2. Gradually add chicken stock, 1/2 cup at a time, and stir until mixture starts to simmer. Season to taste with pepper and cayenne. (At this point sauce can be cooled to room temperature, transferred to serving-size containers, and frozen.)

3. Mix cornstarch with yogurt and add to mixture in saucepan. Reduce heat to low and stir until sauce is thoroughly blended and thickened. Do not boil.

MAKES ABOUT 3 CUPS
APPROXIMATELY 30 MILLIGRAMS SODIUM PER 1/2 CUP

DRESSINGS

Not only are the following dressings far lower in sodium than their commercial counterparts, they're even lower than the low sodium varieties (which average about 25 milligrams of sodium per tablespoon).

For a perfect salad, toss crisp fresh greens and vegetables with any of the dressings that follow. But don't limit them to salads—use them as dips, sauces over steamed vegetables, or with pasta or rice. The vinaigrettes make excellent marinades and basting sauces for broiled or grilled fish, poultry, or vegetables.

LEMON GARLIC VINAIGRETTE

1   clove garlic, pressed
2   teaspoons minced fresh parsley or 1 teaspoon dried
3   tablespoons white wine vinegar
2   tablespoons fresh lemon juice
1/4 cup Low Sodium Chicken Stock (page 3)
1   tablespoon olive oil
2   teaspoons minced pimiento
     Freshly ground pepper to taste

Combine all ingredients in a mixing bowl or jar with a tight-fitting lid. Whisk or cover and shake until thoroughly blended and slightly thickened. Chill for at least 1 hour and stir before serving.

MAKES ABOUT ¾ CUP

APPROXIMATELY 1 MILLIGRAM SODIUM PER TABLESPOON

BALSAMIC VINAIGRETTE

1 small clove garlic, finely minced
2 scallions, white and tender greens, finely sliced
2 tablespoons balsamic vinegar
2 tablespoons red wine vinegar
2 tablespoons water
2 tablespoons olive oil
1 tablespoon minced fresh basil or 1 teaspoon dried
   Freshly ground pepper to taste

Combine all ingredients in a mixing bowl or jar with a tight-fitting lid. Whisk or cover and shake until thoroughly blended and slightly thickened. Chill for at least 1 hour and stir before serving.

MAKES ABOUT ¾ CUP
LESS THAN 1 MILLIGRAM SODIUM PER TABLESPOON

◆ ◆ ◆ ◆ ◆

CREAMY MUSTARD AND HERB DRESSING

▶▶▶▶▶▶▶▶▶▶▶▶▶▶▶▶▶▶▶▶▶▶▶▶▶▶▶

1   medium shallot, finely minced
¼   cup white wine vinegar
¼   cup light sour cream
1   tablespoon vegetable oil
2   teaspoons dry mustard
½   teaspoon dried parsley
½   teaspoon tarragon
½   teaspoon dried dill weed

Combine all ingredients in a mixing bowl or jar with a tight-fitting lid. Whisk or cover and shake until thoroughly blended and slightly thickened. Chill for at least 1 hour and stir before serving.

MAKES ABOUT ¾ CUP
APPROXIMATELY 4 MILLIGRAMS SODIUM PER TABLESPOON

CAESAR-STYLE DRESSING

- 4 ounces soft silken tofu, drained and crumbled
- 1 teaspoon dry mustard
- 3 tablespoons fresh lemon juice
- 1 tablespoon olive oil
- 1 small clove garlic, chopped
- 2 teaspoons grated Parmesan cheese
  Freshly ground pepper to taste

Combine all ingredients in a food processor and process for 5 seconds or until ingredients are smoothly blended. Chill for at least 1 hour before serving.

MAKES ABOUT ³/₄ CUP
APPROXIMATELY 7 MILLIGRAMS SODIUM PER TABLESPOON

CREAMY TOMATO ONION DRESSING

- ¹/₄ cup evaporated skim milk
- ¹/₂ cup no-salt-added low fat cottage cheese
- ¹/₂ small red onion, chopped
- 1 small clove garlic, chopped
- 1 tablespoon fresh lemon juice
- 1 tablespoon minced fresh parsley or basil
  Freshly ground pepper to taste
- 2 ripe plum tomatoes, peeled and minced

1. Combine all ingredients, except 1 tomato, in a food processor and process for 5 seconds or until ingredients are smoothly blended.

2. Transfer dressing to a mixing bowl and stir in remaining tomato. Chill for at least 1 hour before serving.

MAKES ABOUT 1¹/₂ CUPS
APPROXIMATELY 6 MILLIGRAMS SODIUM PER TABLESPOON

APPETIZERS
and
STARTERS

SPICED FISH CAKES

These tangy cakes make an excellent first course. Shaped into tiny balls and speared with toothpicks, they're perfect—and popular—at a party. Try them accompanied by Creamy Tomato Onion Dressing (page 20) or Green Herb Dip (page 33).

$^1/_2$	pound fresh Atlantic cod or scrod fillets
1	medium onion, minced
1	small red bell pepper, seeded and finely minced
$^1/_2$	cup bread crumbs (made from dry white bread)
2	tablespoons minced fresh parsley or cilantro
1	teaspoon ground cumin
1	teaspoon ground cardamom
$^1/_4$	teaspoon cayenne, or to taste
2	large egg whites
	Vegetable oil cooking spray

1. Place fish in a saucepan and cover with unsalted water. Bring water to a boil, reduce heat, and simmer gently until fish is cooked through. Transfer fish and 2 tablespoons of the cooking liquid to a mixing bowl.

2. Flake fish into tiny pieces. Add remaining ingredients, except cooking spray, and toss until thoroughly blended.

3. Heat a large nonstick skillet coated with cooking spray. Place heaping tablespoonfuls of cod mixture in skillet,

making sure that they do not touch one another, and flatten them slightly with the back of a spoon. Cook over medium heat until golden brown on both sides. As they cook, transfer cakes to a heated platter and keep warm. Repeat, adding more cooking spray as needed, until the fish mixture has been used. Serve hot.

MAKES ABOUT 18 FISH CAKES
APPROXIMATELY 20 MILLIGRAMS SODIUM PER FISH CAKE

◆ ◆ ◆ ◆ ◆

SEVICHE

▶ ▶

This Latin American appetizer also makes a light and refreshing summer lunch for four. Don't be put off by the thought of eating raw fish—the fish "cooks" in the marinade.

My recipe uses finfish, in this case sole or flounder, but if you prefer shellfish, scallops make a tasty seviche. Whatever fish you choose, make sure it's very fresh.

1	*pound fresh sole or flounder fillets*
³/₄	*cup fresh lime juice*
	Freshly ground pepper to taste
3	*tablespoons minced red onion*
3	*tablespoons minced red and/or green bell pepper*
2	*teaspoons dried oregano*
4	*tablespoons chopped fresh cilantro*
2	*ripe tomatoes, cut into thin wedges*
1	*medium cucumber, peeled and sliced*

1. Cut fish fillets in half lengthwise, then diagonally into ¹/₂-inch slices. Transfer fish to a glass bowl.

2. Prepare marinade by combining lime juice with ground pepper, onion, bell pepper, oregano, and 2 tablespoons of the cilantro. Stir to blend ingredients thoroughly.

3. Pour marinade over fish and toss gently. Cover and refrigerate, stirring occasionally, for 8 to 10 hours.

4. Just before serving, drain off and discard excess marinade and transfer fish to a serving platter or individual dishes. Sprinkle fish with remaining cilantro and serve surrounded with tomato wedges and cucumber slices.

SERVES 6

APPROXIMATELY 65 MILLIGRAMS SODIUM PER SERVING

◆ ◆ ◆ ◆ ◆

STUFFED MUSHROOMS

▶ ▶

You can also use this spinach stuffing in tomatoes or baked new potatoes, on celery stalks or hearts of artichokes.

12 mushroom caps, about 1¹/₂ inches in diameter, wiped clean
1 teaspoon olive oil
5 ounces fresh spinach, trimmed, rinsed, drained, and shredded
1 large clove garlic, finely minced
   Freshly ground pepper to taste
2 tablespoons light sour cream
2 tablespoons unseasoned bread crumbs, preferably homemade
2 tablespoons freshly grated Parmesan cheese

1. Preheat oven to 400°F.

2. Place mushroom caps, hollow side up, on a nonstick baking sheet and set aside.

3. Heat oil in a nonstick skillet. Add spinach and garlic and cook over medium heat, stirring often, for 10 minutes. Drain off liquid and transfer spinach to a mixing bowl.

4. Add pepper and sour cream to spinach and mix well.

5. Spoon spinach mixture into mushroom caps. Sprinkle top of each cap with ¹/₂ teaspoon bread crumbs and top with ¹/₂ teaspoon grated cheese. Bake for 10 minutes. Serve hot.

MAKES 12 STUFFED MUSHROOMS
APPROXIMATELY 35 MILLIGRAMS SODIUM PER MUSHROOM

◆ ◆ ◆ ◆ ◆

TZATZIKI

▶ ▶

Called *tzatziki* in Greece, *cacik* in Turkey, and *mast 'o' khrat* in Iran, this popular Mideastern salad is traditionally served as a side dish with rice and meat. Accompanied by chilled raw vegetables or hot pita, it makes an excellent appetizer or light lunch. Whatever you call it and however you serve it, this tasty yogurt and cucumber salad is low in fat, cholesterol, and calories as well as sodium.

There are many recipes for this dish; my version uses paprika in place of salt, which also imparts a pleasing color.

12 *ounces low fat plain yogurt*
2 *medium cucumbers, peeled, seeded, and chopped*
2 *cloves garlic, finely minced*
4 *teaspoons chopped fresh mint or 2 teaspoons
    dried*
1 *teaspoon paprika, or more to taste*

Combine all ingredients and stir gently to blend. Transfer to a serving dish, dust lightly with additional paprika if desired, and chill for at least 1 hour before serving.

MAKES ABOUT 3 CUPS
APPROXIMATELY 45 MILLIGRAMS SODIUM PER ½ CUP

◆ ◆ ◆ ◆ ◆

SHRIMP-STUFFED CHERRY TOMATOES

▶ ▶

If large cherry tomatoes are unavailable, substitute four medium just-ripe tomatoes.

12	*large ripe cherry tomatoes, about 1¹/₂ inches in diameter*
¹/₄	*pound shrimp, cooked, shelled, deveined, and chopped*
¹/₄	*cup minced green bell pepper*
¹/₄	*cup peeled, seeded, and chopped cucumber*
2	*tablespoons minced red onion*
2	*tablespoons minced fresh cilantro*
2	*tablespoons red wine vinegar*
2	*teaspoons olive oil*
	Freshly ground pepper to taste

1. Slice off tops of tomatoes. Leaving shells intact, carefully scoop out seeds and pulp and transfer pulp to a mixing bowl. Set shells aside.

2. Add remaining ingredients to bowl and mix until well blended.

3. Spoon mixture into tomato shells, letting stuffing overflow slightly. Chill before serving.

MAKES 12 STUFFED CHERRY TOMATOES
APPROXIMATELY 18 MILLIGRAMS SODIUM PER TOMATO

◆ ◆ ◆ ◆ ◆

CREAMY CURRIED BEAN SPREAD

▶ ▶

Be sure to use cooked, not canned, beans. A cup of cooked white beans contains only 12 milligrams of sodium, compared to the 1,200 milligrams in the canned variety!

To prepare the beans, just soak them overnight in lots of unsalted water, drain, then cook the beans in fresh (again, unsalted) water until they are tender.

1   *cup cooked and drained white beans*
2   *tablespoons cider vinegar or fresh lemon juice*
¹/₄   *cup Low Sodium Chicken Stock (page 3)*
1   *tablespoon ginger root, freshly minced*
1   *tablespoon mild or hot curry powder, or to taste*
    Freshly ground pepper to taste
¹/₄   *cup low fat plain yogurt*
1   *scallion, white and tender greens, minced*

1. Combine beans with remaining ingredients, except yogurt and scallions, in a food processor and process until beans are blended to a smooth paste.

2. With processor running, slowly add yogurt and process until thoroughly combined.

3. Transfer bean mixture to a serving bowl and sprinkle with scallions. Serve chilled or at room temperature.

MAKES ABOUT 1³/₄ CUPS
APPROXIMATELY 4 MILLIGRAMS SODIUM PER TABLESPOON

◆ ◆ ◆ ◆ ◆

FOUR FABULOUS DIPS

► ►

The best way to serve dips is with a platter of cool, crunchy fresh vegetables, either raw or steamed to the crisp-tender stage. Arrange the vegetables attractively on a serving platter, varying colors, sizes, and shapes. Have the dip or dips (two or three different ones are nice) readily accessible.

The vegetables listed below make ideal accompaniments to any of the dips that follow. Their approximate sodium content is included because you'll want to take that into account.

sodium milligrams per ounce

Asparagus, steamed spears	1
Bell pepper (green, red, yellow), raw strips	1
Broccoli, raw or steamed florets	8
Bok choy (Chinese cabbage), raw sticks	19
Carrots, raw sticks	10
Cauliflower, raw or steamed florets	4
Celery, raw sticks	25
Cherry tomatoes, raw	3
Cucumber, raw slices	1
Green beans, steamed whole	2
Mushrooms, raw caps	1
Pea pods (sugar, snap, or snow), raw or steamed	1
Radish, raw whole or sliced	7
Scallions, raw small whole or halved	5
Zucchini, raw strips	1

♦ ♦ ♦ ♦ ♦

DILLED CHEESE DIP

▶ ▶

1   cup no-salt-added low fat cottage cheese
2   tablespoons minced fresh dill weed or 1
    tablespoon dried
3   tablespoons minced scallions
2   tablespoons diced pimiento
    Freshly ground pepper to taste

Combine all ingredients and stir to blend thoroughly.
Cover and refrigerate for at least 1 hour before serving.

MAKES ABOUT 1⅓ CUPS

APPROXIMATELY 4 MILLIGRAMS SODIUM PER TABLESPOON

◆ ◆ ◆ ◆ ◆

GREEN HERB DIP

▶ ▶

This makes a delicious dip, but it's also an excellent sauce for broiled or grilled fish or seafood, and it's the ideal accompaniment for cold poached fish.

$1/2$	pound fresh spinach, trimmed, rinsed, steamed, and well drained
$1/2$	cup tightly packed watercress
$1/4$	cup tightly packed fresh parsley
1	clove garlic, chopped
1	large shallot, chopped
$1/2$	teaspoon celery seed
1	teaspoon dry mustard
1	teaspoon dried tarragon
3	tablespoons light low sodium mayonnaise
$1/4$	cup light sour cream
2	teaspoons wine vinegar
	Freshly ground pepper to taste

1. Combine spinach, watercress, parsley, garlic, and shallot in a food processor and process until coarsely pureed. Transfer to a mixing bowl.

2. Combine remaining ingredients and mix well. Add to spinach mixture and stir until thoroughly blended. Chill for at least 1 hour before serving.

MAKES ABOUT 2 CUPS
APPROXIMATELY 10 MILLIGRAMS SODIUM PER TABLESPOON

◆ ◆ ◆ ◆ ◆

SUN-DRIED TOMATO DIP

▶ ▶

8	no-salt-added sun-dried tomato halves (*not oil packed*)
1	cup boiling water
1	clove garlic, chopped
1	small onion, chopped
¼	cup low fat ricotta cheese
½	cup All-Purpose Tomato Sauce (*page 9*) or canned low sodium tomato sauce
	Dash hot pepper sauce, or to taste
1	tablespoon minced fresh basil or parsley

1. Soak sun-dried tomatoes in boiling water for 5 minutes or until softened. Let cool slightly, then drain and coarsely chop.

2. Combine tomatoes with remaining ingredients, except basil or parsley, in a food processor and process for 10 seconds or until smoothly blended.

3. Transfer to a serving bowl and sprinkle lightly with basil or parsley. Serve chilled or at room temperature.

MAKES ABOUT 1 CUP

APPROXIMATELY 7 MILLIGRAMS SODIUM PER TABLESPOON

BLUE CHEESE DIP

This dip doubles as a fabulous filling for raw or crisp-steamed snow pea pods.

$^3/_4$ ounce blue cheese, crumbled

$^3/_4$ cup no-salt-added low fat cottage cheese

1 teaspoon dry mustard

2 tablespoons white wine vinegar

$^1/_2$ teaspoon mild or hot paprika

1. Combine all ingredients, except paprika, in a food processor and process until smoothly blended.

2. Transfer to a serving bowl, sprinkle with paprika, and chill for at least 1 hour before serving.

MAKES ABOUT 1 CUP

APPROXIMATELY 23 MILLIGRAMS SODIUM PER TABLESPOON

SOUPS
and
CHOWDERS

◆◆◆◆◆

CHICKEN VEGETABLE SOUP
WITH SHELLS

▶▶▶▶▶▶▶▶▶▶▶▶▶▶▶▶▶▶▶▶▶▶▶▶▶

I am convinced that many of the best soups are impromptu creations culled from scraps in the refrigerator and the bounty from the garden or greengrocer's shelf.

I devise my soup recipes by using favorite combinations. Like a woman possessed, I storm the aisles. I sniff, I tear off a leaf and taste, I buy what's appealing. With the addition of fresh-snipped or pinched-dried herbs, a few grinds of the pepper mill, the starch of choice, poultry or meat for a splurge, *voilà!*—soup's on, and ready to be enjoyed!

This recipe, which combines fresh vegetables, chicken, and pasta, is a good example of a soup low in sodium and fat but rich in complex carbohydrates, vitamins, and flavor.

2	teaspoons vegetable oil
1	medium onion, chopped
1	stalk celery, diced
1	small green bell pepper, cored, seeded, and diced
2	carrots, diced
2	ripe plum tomatoes, coarsely chopped
1	cup dry white table wine
3	cups Low Sodium Chicken Stock (page 3)
8	ounces white chicken meat, cubed
2	tablespoons chopped fresh basil or 1 tablespoon dried
	Freshly ground pepper to taste
3/4	cup uncooked small pasta shells

1. Heat oil in a large nonstick stockpot. Add onion, celery, and green pepper and cook over low heat, stirring often, for 5 minutes or until onion is translucent.

2. Add carrots and tomatoes and simmer over low heat, stirring often, for an additional 5 minutes.

3. Add remaining ingredients, except pasta shells, and stir to combine. Bring to a low boil, then cover, reduce heat, and simmer gently for 10 minutes.

4. Add pasta shells. Cover and continue to simmer over low heat for about 15 minutes or until vegetables are tender and pasta is cooked.

SERVES 4

APPROXIMATELY 90 MILLIGRAMS SODIUM PER SERVING

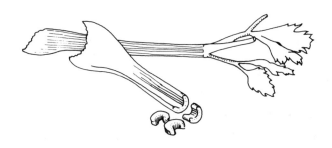

SPLIT PEA AND TOMATO SOUP

Every Sunday around 4:00 in the afternoon, our neighbors the Bottoms used to set out a sumptuous supper centered around a whole cured ham with all the trimmings. And by 7:30 that evening this behemoth porker would be devoured.

With the same clockwork regularity, Monday's meal always used the remnants of that humongous ham: its bone and the attached shards of meat. The result was a glorious, soothing split pea soup. Creamy and rich in salt, whoever shared this quasi-religious experience carried the resultant puffy eyes as a culinary cross to bear. How blissfully ignorant we were of the bloat-causing culprit—salt.

Today, Monday nights mean football and friends for dinner. I serve this beautiful rendition of split pea soup, sans the salt, with memorable results.

2	teaspoons olive oil
2	medium onions, chopped
1	stalk celery, chopped
2	cloves garlic, finely minced
3	ripe plum tomatoes, chopped
1/4	cup chopped fresh parsley
1	teaspoon dried thyme
1	teaspoon dried rosemary
	Freshly ground pepper to taste
3/4	cup dried split peas
5	cups water

1. Heat oil in a large nonstick stockpot. Add onions, celery, and garlic and cook over medium heat until onion is translucent.

2. Stir in tomatoes, parsley, thyme, rosemary, and pepper. Add split peas and water. Cover and simmer over very low heat, stirring occasionally, for about 2 hours or until peas are tender. Add additional water if soup becomes too thick.

SERVES 4

APPROXIMATELY 20 MILLIGRAMS SODIUM PER SERVING

HEARTY BEEF SOUP WITH ORZO

Orzo, also called *rosamarina*, is a tiny rice-shaped pasta you will find on the pasta shelf of your supermarket or grocery store. Long a favorite in Greek and Italian cuisines, orzo is gaining popularity with American foodies as well. Great as a thickener for soups, it is also a tasty and attractive alternative to potatoes or rice.

$1/2$ pound lean stewing beef, cut into $1/2$-inch cubes
2 cups water
3 cups Low Sodium Beef Stock (page 5)
1 cup dry red table wine
   Freshly ground pepper to taste
1 bay leaf, crumbled
$1/4$ cup minced fresh parsley
2 onions, coarsely chopped
1 large stalk celery, chopped or sliced
2 small turnips, peeled and cubed
2 carrots, sliced
$1/2$ cup uncooked orzo

1. Combine beef, water, stock, wine, pepper, bay leaf, parsley, onions, and celery in a large stockpot and bring to a boil. Cover, reduce heat, and simmer gently for 1 hour.

2. Add turnips and carrots, cover and simmer for 30 minutes or until beef is tender and vegetables are cooked.

3. Add orzo, cover and simmer for an additional 15 minutes or until orzo is tender.

SERVES **4**

APPROXIMATELY **95** MILLIGRAMS SODIUM PER SERVING

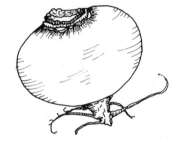

◆ ◆ ◆ ◆ ◆

CORN AND RED PEPPER CHOWDER

▶ ▶

In the early days of colonization the vigorous settlers of New England created a bounty of good thick soups called chowders. These chowders were the American version of Old World potages, originally made with milk and fish. As vegetables abounded in home gardens, chowders evolved to include vegetable-milk combinations.

The demand today is for lighter, healthier fare that doesn't sacrifice flavor. This lovely chowder fills the bill with flair and style.

2	*medium potatoes, peeled and cubed*
1	*teaspoon vegetable oil*
1	*large onion, diced*
1	*stalk celery, diced*
1	*medium red bell pepper, seeded and diced*
2	*tablespoons chopped fresh parsley*
1	*teaspoon dried marjoram*
$^{1}/_{2}$	*teaspoon dried tarragon*
	Freshly ground pepper to taste
2	*cups low fat (2%) milk*
2	*cups Low Sodium Vegetable Stock (page 7)*
2	*cups corn kernels, fresh or frozen and thawed*

1. In a large stockpot, boil potatoes in unsalted water until barely tender; do not overcook. Remove from heat, drain potatoes, and reserve 1 cup of cooking liquid. Return potatoes to pot and set aside.

2. Heat oil in a nonstick skillet. Add onion, celery, red pepper, parsley, marjoram, tarragon, and pepper to taste. Cook over low heat, stirring often, for 3 minutes or until onions are just tender. Add contents of skillet to potatoes in pot.

3. Add reserved potato liquid, milk, stock, and corn to pot, stir, and cook over medium heat until soup starts to simmer. Cover, reduce heat to very low, and simmer gently for 10 minutes.

SERVES 4

APPROXIMATELY 95 MILLIGRAMS SODIUM PER SERVING

♦ ♦ ♦ ♦ ♦

LENTIL SOUP WITH POTATOES

▶ ▶

Also known as *pulses*, legumes are the seeds of plants that have pods. They are rich in vitamins and proteins, low in fat, contain no cholesterol, and are very filling in small quantities. While this country has been a little sluggish in adopting this fabulous food, legumes are an indispensable commodity in kitchens of India and the countries of the Middle East, the Mediterranean, Africa, and South America.

Legumes such as beans, peas, and lentils are served cold in salads or hot in stews, side dishes, and soups like this one.

2	teaspoons vegetable oil
1	large onion, finely minced
2	cloves garlic, finely minced
3/4	cup dry lentils, rinsed and picked over
4	cups water
2	cups Low Sodium Chicken Stock (page 3) or Low Sodium Beef Stock (page 5)
1/2	cup dry white table wine
1	large potato, peeled and cut into 1-inch cubes
1	teaspoon dried thyme
1	bay leaf, crumbled
	Freshly ground pepper to taste
1	tablespoon dry sherry (not cooking sherry)

1. Heat oil in a large nonstick stockpot. Add onion and garlic and cook over medium-high heat until lightly browned.

2. Add all remaining ingredients, except sherry, and bring to a boil. Cover, reduce heat to low, and simmer gently, stirring occasionally, for 45 minutes or until lentils are tender.

3. Stir in sherry and cook for an additional 2 minutes.

SERVES 4

APPROXIMATELY 20 MILLIGRAMS SODIUM PER SERVING

SPINACH AND KALE SOUP
WITH WILD RICE

▶ ▶

One of my favorite ways of presenting a robust soup such as this one is in a large, sturdy stoneware or pottery mixing bowl, dished up with a wooden ladle. And if I'm serving a substantial soup for lunch, I may use some funky mugs or oversized cups and saucers.

For a *souper* lunch or light dinner, serve with a sandwich on good grainy bread or with a side salad and a light dessert.

$3/4$ cup uncooked wild rice
5 cups water
1 tablespoon red wine vinegar
1 teaspoon vegetable oil
2 onions, chopped
6 ounces fresh kale, trimmed, rinsed, and chopped
10 ounces fresh spinach, trimmed, rinsed, drained, and chopped or shredded
$1^{1}/2$ cups All-Purpose Tomato Sauce (page 9)
Freshly ground pepper to taste

1. In a large stockpot, cover rice with water, add vinegar, and bring to a boil. Reduce heat to low and simmer gently for 30 minutes.

2. Meanwhile, heat oil in a nonstick skillet and sauté onions until lightly browned. Stir in kale and spinach and cook over medium heat, stirring occasionally, for about 10 minutes or until kale is cooked.

3. Drain off any excess liquid from kale-spinach mixture and stir in tomato sauce and pepper to taste.

4. Add contents of skillet to rice and liquid in pot. Stir, cover, and cook over low heat, stirring occasionally, for 15 minutes or until rice is fully cooked.

SERVES **4**

APPROXIMATELY **75** MILLIGRAMS SODIUM PER SERVING

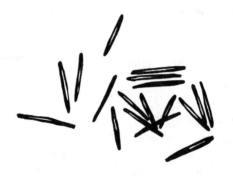

◆ ◆ ◆ ◆ ◆

SPICED SEAFOOD CHOWDER

▶ ▶

The first great seafood chowder I ever tasted was a velvety masterpiece composed at a huge, cavernous fish house called Lundy Bros. in Sheepshead Bay, Brooklyn, New York. Their Boston clam chowder consisted of littleneck clams, gargantuan chunks of potatoes, celery, and carrots, and flecks of pimiento, all heaped in a bath of heavy cream covered by a thin veil of paprika. It was Nirvana.

The years have passed, as has Lundy Bros., and with them my taste for excessive salt. But my love of seafood chowders remains in all its Proustian splendor. And this zesty clamless and creamless version has made many of my feasts special.

2¹/₂	cups water
¹/₂	pound Atlantic cod fillets
12	medium shrimp, shelled and deveined
12	small scallops or 6 large quartered
2	medium potatoes, peeled and cubed
1	stalk celery, chopped
1	large onion, chopped
2	tablespoons diced pimientos
2¹/₂	cups Spicy Tomato Sauce (page 11)
¹/₂	cup dry white table wine
¹/₄	cup chopped fresh parsley or cilantro
1	teaspoon dried oregano
	Hot red pepper flakes to taste

1. In a large stockpot bring water to a boil, lower heat, and add cod, shrimp, and scallops. Cook over medium heat for 3 minutes. With a slotted spoon, remove fish and shellfish and set aside, reserving liquid in pot.

2. Add remaining ingredients to liquid in pot and cook over low heat, partially covered, stirring occasionally, for 15 minutes or until potatoes are tender.

3. Return fish and shellfish to pot and stir over medium heat for 2 minutes.

SERVES 4

APPROXIMATELY 130 MILLIGRAMS SODIUM PER SERVING

♦ ♦ ♦ ♦ ♦

CREAMY WATERCRESS SOUP

▶ ▶

When preparing a soup consisting of stock or broth—whether it be vegetable, beef, or chicken as in this soup—the good taste of the soup will depend largely on the quality of the stock. I always use my own stocks, which are low in fat as well as in sodium, and keep several containers in the freezer.

2	teaspoons unsalted butter or margarine, or blend
1	onion, minced
1	large bunch watercress, rinsed and coarsely chopped
3½	cups Low Sodium Chicken Stock (page 3)
1	large potato, peeled and cut into ½-inch cubes Freshly ground pepper to taste
1	cup low fat (2%) milk
3	tablespoons light sour cream
4	sprigs watercress for garnish

1. Heat butter or margarine in a large nonstick skillet. Add onion and cook over medium heat for about 3 minutes or until onion is translucent.

2. Stir in chopped watercress, 1 cup of stock, and the potato. Cover, reduce heat, and simmer gently for 15 minutes or until potato is tender.

3. Transfer contents of skillet to a blender or food processor and blend for 10 seconds or until ingredients are smoothly pureed.

4. Transfer watercress mixture to a large stockpot, stir in remaining stock, and add pepper to taste. Bring to a simmer over medium heat, then cover, reduce heat, and simmer gently for 5 minutes, stirring occasionally.

5. Stir in milk and cook, uncovered, over very low heat until soup is hot but not boiling. Remove from heat and stir in sour cream. Serve hot or chilled, garnished with reserved watercress sprigs.

SERVES 4

APPROXIMATELY 90 MILLIGRAMS SODIUM PER SERVING

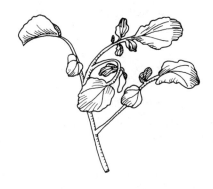

FRENCH ONION SOUP

Soon after Labor Day has passed and the welcome air of autumn approaches, I yield to an overwhelming desire for a brown crock brimming with fragrant onion soup. For me there is no greater harbinger of the cool months to come than this glorious brew steeping in a cauldron on my kitchen stove.

This low sodium version of the French classic makes a lusty meal when accompanied by a crisp green salad tossed with Caesar-style Dressing (page 19) and a selection of fresh fruit—*c'est bon!*

2	teaspoons unsalted butter or margarine, or blend
4	medium onions, thinly sliced
2	teaspoons minced garlic
1	teaspoon sugar
1	tablespoon flour
5	cups Low Sodium Beef Stock (page 5)
$^1/_2$	cup dry white table wine
	Freshly ground pepper to taste
4	very thin slices French bread, dried or toasted
$^1/_2$	clove garlic
2	tablespoons grated Parmesan cheese

1. Melt butter or margarine in a large stockpot. Add onions and cook over low heat, stirring often, until onions are golden. Add garlic and stir briefly.

2. Sprinkle onions and garlic with sugar and flour and stir over low heat for 2 minutes or until blended.

3. Add stock, wine, and pepper to taste. Bring to a boil, then reduce heat and simmer gently, partially covered, for 20 minutes.

4. Preheat broiler while soup simmers.

5. Ladle soup into 4 ovenproof serving bowls. Rub garlic half over both sides of bread slices. Float a slice of bread in each bowl and sprinkle each with ½ tablespoon of grated Parmesan cheese. Place bowls in oven, about 3 inches from heat source, and broil for about 3 minutes or until bread is lightly browned.

SERVES 4

APPROXIMATELY 150 MILLIGRAMS SODIUM PER SERVING

♦ ♦ ♦ ♦ ♦

ASPARAGUS FENNEL SOUP

▶ ▶

If you like asparagus and fennel, this combination will be a pleasant and flavorful surprise. The potato gives the soup body and adds its own satisfying taste. Serve hot or chilled.

1   *pound fresh asparagus*
1   *small fennel bulb, trimmed and chopped*
1   *small onion, chopped*
1   *medium potato, peeled and diced*
1   *cup water*
3   *cups Low Sodium Chicken Stock (page 3)*
1   *cup evaporated low fat milk*
    Freshly ground pepper to taste

1. Bend asparagus stems until they snap at the natural point between the tough and tender parts. Discard tough stalk ends or reserve for another purpose. Cut off 8 asparagus tips and set aside. Cut remaining asparagus into 1-inch pieces.

2. In a large stockpot, combine asparagus with fennel, onion, potato, water, and stock and bring to a boil. Cover, reduce heat to low, and simmer gently for 20 minutes or until vegetables are very tender.

3. While soup simmers, combine reserved asparagus tips with a little boiling water in a small saucepan and cook for 2 minutes or until just crisp-tender. Drain and set tips aside.

4. Transfer soup mixture to a food processor and blend for 5 seconds or until vegetables are coarsely pureed (if necessary, do this in several batches).

5. Return pureed soup to pot, stir in milk, and add pepper to taste. If serving soup chilled, cool to room temperature, then refrigerate for 30 minutes before serving. If serving soup hot, stir over very low heat until soup begins to simmer. Either way, garnish each serving with reserved asparagus tips.

SERVES 4

APPROXIMATELY 90 MILLIGRAMS SODIUM PER SERVING

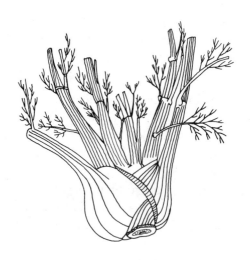

◆ ◆ ◆ ◆ ◆

GAZPACHO

▶ ▶

In this low sodium interpretation of the "summer salad soup" of Mexico, most of the vegetables are finely chopped. If you prefer a smooth gazpacho, puree all the vegetables in a food processor.

If you don't like green pepper (or if it doesn't like you), eliminate it and adjust the amounts of other vegetables.

For a touch of elegance, you might present this beautiful-looking soup in balloon goblets and pass small dishes of extra chopped vegetables, hard-cooked egg whites, or unsalted croutons.

2   *ripe plum tomatoes, chopped*
1   *small onion, quartered*
2   *cloves garlic, chopped*
2   *teaspoons olive oil*
2   *tablespoons fresh lemon juice*
    Freshly ground pepper to taste
2   *tablespoons minced fresh parsley or cilantro*
    Dash hot pepper sauce (optional)
3   *cups Low Sodium Chicken Stock (page 3) or Low Sodium Vegetable Stock (page 7)*
1   *small green bell pepper, seeded*
1   *medium cucumber, peeled and seeded*
1   *small zucchini, peeled and seeded*
4   *scallions, white and tender greens, chopped*

1. In a large blender or food processor, combine tomatoes, onion, garlic, oil, lemon juice, ground pepper, parsley or

cilantro, hot pepper sauce if desired, and 1 cup of stock. Process until ingredients are thoroughly blended. Transfer to a large serving bowl or soup tureen and set aside.

2. Mince green pepper, cucumber, zucchini, and scallions. Add to tomato mixture in bowl or tureen and stir in remaining stock. Chill for at least 2 hours and stir well before serving.

SERVES 4

APPROXIMATELY 25 MILLIGRAMS SODIUM PER SERVING

◆◆◆◆◆

CHILLED YOGURT AND MELON SOUP

▶▶▶▶▶▶▶▶▶▶▶▶▶▶▶▶▶▶▶▶▶▶▶▶

My friend Jennifer believes yogurt is the supreme health food: prolonging life, fortifying the body, and conferring good looks. Jen applies it to her skin when sunburned and as a nighttime facial mask. Me? I enjoy it as a food, whether blended with fruits, as a dressing for salad, or heaped on baked potatoes with a pinch of dry mustard or fresh herbs.

This cool and different yogurt and melon soup is a perfect way to start a summertime dinner.

Pulp from 5-inch-diameter cantaloupe, cubed
1   medium cucumber, peeled, seeded, and chopped
1   tablespoon chopped fresh mint or 2 teaspoons dried
1½ cups low fat plain yogurt
¾   cup cranberry juice
Mint leaves for garnish

1. Combine all ingredients in a large blender or food processor and process until smoothly pureed (do this in several batches if necessary).

2. Transfer mixture to a large mixing bowl. Cover and refrigerate for at least 2 hours, stirring occasionally.

3. Remove from refrigerator, stir well, and ladle into a tureen or individual bowls. Garnish with mint leaves and serve.

SERVES 4
APPROXIMATELY 75 MILLIGRAMS SODIUM PER SERVING

MEATS

◆ ◆ ◆ ◆ ◆

PEPPERED BEEF STEW IN RED WINE

▶ ▶

Stews are a boon to hosts and hostesses because they're relatively easy to prepare, can accommodate any number of guests, can be cooked in advance and reheated, and may be tailored to suit individual tastes or whims.

If you feel like adding vegetables to this beef stew, go right ahead, but do so about a half hour before the meat is done. Use pearl onions, small peeled potatoes, diced turnips, or baby carrots in any combination you prefer, remembering to figure in their sodium content.

3	teaspoons vegetable oil
1	pound boneless top round, trimmed of all visible fat and cut into 1-inch cubes
2	teaspoons coarsely ground fresh pepper, or to taste
$1/2$	cup chopped fresh parsley
1	bay leaf
1	large onion, diced
1	stalk celery with top, chopped
2	cloves garlic, finely minced
6	large mushrooms, wiped clean, stems removed, sliced
1	tablespoon all-purpose flour
$1^{1}/_{2}$	cups water
1	cup dry red table wine

1. Preheat oven to 350°F.
2. Heat 2 teaspoons oil in a large nonstick skillet and

brown beef on all sides over medium-high heat. Using a slotted spoon, transfer beef to a large ovenproof casserole, sprinkle with pepper and parsley, add bay leaf, and set aside.

3. Add onion, celery, and garlic to skillet and cook over low heat until onion is translucent. With a slotted spoon, transfer vegetables to casserole with beef.

4. Heat remaining teaspoon oil in skillet, add mushrooms, and cook over low heat, stirring often, for 2 minutes. Dissolve flour in water, add to skillet, and stir over low heat until mixture begins to thicken. Stir in wine and simmer for 1 minute.

5. Transfer contents of skillet to casserole and stir gently to blend ingredients. Cover and bake for 1½ hours or until meat is tender. Stir occasionally and add a little water if too much liquid evaporates.

SERVES 4

APPROXIMATELY 130 MILLIGRAMS SODIUM PER SERVING

♦ ♦ ♦ ♦ ♦

GLAZED BRISKET OF BEEF

▶ ▶

Here's a feast to satisfy the most finicky dinner guest or family member.

Brisket is a tasty cut of beef, but it's also fatty. The fat content can be greatly reduced if you use the leaner thin-cut or flat end, trim the visible fat before cooking, and discard the accumulated fat after the brisket is cooked.

After cooking, place the brisket on a hot serving platter and surround the sliced meat with steamed asparagus or French-cut green beans and small new potatoes brushed lightly with olive oil and cooked to a golden brown. Or try it with brown rice and Creamy Broccoli Puree (page 169).

2	pounds fresh lean brisket, flat end (thin cut), trimmed of all visible fat
1	large onion, coarsely diced
1	stalk celery, chopped
2	cloves garlic, coarsely minced
1/4	cup chopped fresh parsley
	Freshly ground pepper to taste
2	teaspoons brown sugar
2	teaspoons dry mustard
1	tablespoon cider vinegar
3	tablespoons dry red table wine

1. Preheat oven to 350°F.

2. Place brisket, flat side down, in a baking pan. Add water to a depth of 1 inch. Surround brisket with onion,

celery, and garlic, and sprinkle with parsley and pepper. Cover and bake for about 2 hours or until brisket is just tender. Remove cover and bake for an additional 15 minutes.

3. Combine sugar and mustard with vinegar and stir until blended into a smooth paste, adding more vinegar if needed.

4. Remove brisket from oven and raise oven temperature to 400°F. Pour off pan juices into a dish and refrigerate. Brush top of brisket with sugar-mustard mixture and add 2 tablespoons water to the baking pan. Return brisket to oven and roast, uncovered, for about 15 minutes or until brisket is browned and glazed. When brisket is done, transfer to a cutting board and let stand for 5 minutes.

5. While brisket stands, skim off and discard all surface fat from chilled pan juices. Strain remaining juices into a saucepan, add wine, and simmer for 5 minutes.

6. Cut brisket against the grain into thin slices, transfer to a heated serving platter, spoon a little of the hot pan juices over slices, and serve accompanied with remaining pan juices.

SERVES 6
APPROXIMATELY 123 MILLIGRAMS SODIUM PER SERVING

◆ ◆ ◆ ◆ ◆

CHOLENT

▶ ▶

Ⓒholent, a beef roast potted with beans, barley, and vegetables, is a one-dish meal traditionally served on the Jewish Sabbath. Because religious beliefs forbid Orthodox Jews to light a fire on the Sabbath, all the ingredients are gathered together the day before and placed in a warm (usually 200°F.) oven to simmer very, very slowly—often for up to 24 hours. When the Cholent is presented at the Sabbath table, the ingredients have been integrated into a welcome and satisfying midday feast.

My version doesn't require a full day in the oven, but it does simmer very slowly, which gives the dish its characteristic richness of flavor. And, as a cost-saving bonus, the slow cooking allows less expensive cuts of meat, such as chuck, to tenderize fully.

1   tablespoon vegetable oil
    Vegetable oil cooking spray
2   pounds chuck roast, trimmed of all visible fat
2   large onions, diced
4   cloves garlic, coarsely chopped
1   tablespoon paprika
1   teaspoon ground ginger
1   bay leaf
1   cup Low Sodium Beef Stock (page 5)
1   cup dried lima beans, picked over, rinsed,
    soaked overnight in unsalted water, and
    drained
4   medium carrots, cut into 1-inch lengths

6 medium potatoes, peeled and quartered
$^1/_2$ cup uncooked barley
Freshly ground pepper to taste

1. Heat oil in a large, ovenproof kettle coated lightly with cooking spray. Add beef and brown on all sides over medium-high heat. Remove beef from pot and set aside.

2. Add onions to pot (coat with a little additional cooking spray if needed) and sauté over medium-high heat, stirring often, until onions are browned but not burned.

3. Reduce heat to low and add garlic. Sprinkle with paprika and ginger, stir to blend, and add bay leaf and stock. Simmer for 2 minutes to blend ingredients. Remove pot from heat.

4. Place beef on top of onion mixture along with any accumulated juices. Surround beef with lima beans, carrots, potatoes, and barley, and season with pepper to taste. Pour in enough water to just cover ingredients, and stir gently. Return pot to heat and bring to a boil. Reduce heat and simmer gently for 20 minutes.

5. Preheat oven to 250°F.

6. Cover pot and bake about 6 hours, stirring occasionally and adding more water if too much liquid evaporates.

7. Transfer beef to a cutting board and let stand for 5 minutes. With a sharp knife, cut beef into thin slices and place on a heated serving platter. Using a slotted spoon, surround beef with vegetables, beans, and barley. Spoon on a little sauce and serve accompanied with any leftover sauce from the pot.

SERVES 6

APPROXIMATELY 97 MILLIGRAMS SODIUM PER SERVING

VEAL SCALOPPINE IN LEMON PARSLEY SAUCE

▶ ▶

In the best of all possible worlds, all scaloppine would be cut across the grain from the top round. Your perfect butcher would happily agree to cut them just a touch over 1/4 inch thick and he or she would flatten them to just a touch under 1/4 inch. In the best of worlds everything is possible—even finding agreeable butchers. But in the real world, most of us will have to pound our veal with our own mallets, cleavers, heavy skillets, or what have you until we attain the wisps of veal we so desire.

This exquisite scaloppine in lemon and parsley sauce is a classic and one you will enjoy many times. But be forewarned: this dish cooks in a hurry and must be tended to or you'll wind up with Frisbee scaloppine. (Fillet of sole makes an elegant stand-in for the veal.)

1	pound veal cutlets, trimmed of all visible fat
2	tablespoons flour
2	teaspoons olive oil
1	small clove garlic, minced
1 1/2	tablespoons fresh lemon juice
1/2	cup dry white table wine
1/4	cup loosely packed, finely chopped fresh parsley
	Freshly ground pepper to taste
	Lemon wedges and parsley sprigs for garnish

1. Pound veal cutlets between sheets of wax paper to a thickness of about ¼ inch. Dredge veal in flour and shake off excess.

2. Heat oil in a large nonstick skillet. Add veal to skillet and cook over medium-high heat for 1 minute per side or until veal is lightly browned and just cooked through. Remove veal to a heated serving platter and keep warm.

3. Reduce heat to medium, add garlic, and stir until lightly golden. Add lemon juice to skillet, and stir, scraping up any browned bits. Stir in wine, parsley, and pepper to taste. Bring to a boil, then reduce heat to low and simmer gently, stirring, for 2 minutes.

4. Spoon lemon parsley sauce over veal, garnish with lemon wedges and parsley sprigs, and serve.

SERVES 4

APPROXIMATELY 103 MILLIGRAMS SODIUM PER SERVING

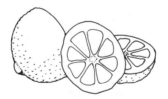

VEAL-STUFFED ZUCCHINI

Serve this flavorful dish with your favorite pasta and a salad of mixed seasonal greens.

	Vegetable oil cooking spray
4	medium zucchini, each about 8 inches long, ends trimmed
2	teaspoons olive oil
1	small onion, minced
1	clove garlic, minced
3/4	pound lean ground veal
1	teaspoon dried thyme
	Freshly ground pepper to taste
1	cup All-Purpose Tomato Sauce (page 9)
	Dash hot pepper sauce (optional)
8	teaspoons grated sharp cheddar cheese

1. Preheat oven to 350°F. Coat surface of a shallow baking pan with cooking spray and set aside.

2. Cook zucchini in boiling, unsalted water for 5 minutes. Drain and let cool slightly.

3. Cut zucchini in half lengthwise. Carefully scoop out pulp, leaving about 1/4 inch of shells intact. Set pulp and shells aside.

4. Heat oil in a nonstick skillet. Add onion and garlic and cook over low heat, stirring often, for 2 minutes. Add ground veal and cook over high heat, stirring and separating clumps of meat, for 5 minutes. Remove from heat and tip

skillet to drain off any fat. Stir in zucchini pulp and cook for an additional 2 minutes.

5. Sprinkle with thyme and pepper, and add ½ cup tomato sauce and hot pepper sauce if desired. Stir over high heat for 3 minutes.

6. Place the 8 zucchini shells, side by side, in prepared baking pan. Spoon meat mixture into shells. Spoon 1 tablespoon of remaining tomato sauce over meat mixture in each shell and sprinkle each with a teaspoon of grated cheddar cheese. Bake for 20 minutes. Serve hot.

SERVES 4

APPROXIMATELY 113 MILLIGRAMS SODIUM PER SERVING

ROAST LEG OF LAMB
ROLLED WITH SPINACH

▶▶▶▶▶▶▶▶▶▶▶▶▶▶▶▶▶▶▶▶▶▶▶▶▶▶▶

This is an ideal entrée for a special dinner party. A spiral of green spinach contrasts beautifully with the red (for rare) or pink (for medium) of the lamb.

A six-pound leg may seem like a lot, but it will weigh less after deboning. In addition, my recipe calls for trimming all visible fat before cooking and skimming all fat from the pan juices after cooking.

6	*pound leg of lamb, boned and butterflied but not tied*
4	*cloves garlic, finely minced*
1	*teaspoon dried rosemary*
	Freshly ground pepper to taste
2	*teaspoons olive oil*
1	*medium onion, minced*
10	*ounces fresh or frozen spinach, chopped and well drained*
1	*cup unseasoned bread crumbs (made from dry or toasted white bread)*
1	*tablespoon flour*
3/4	*cup water*
1/4	*cup dry red or white table wine*

1. Preheat oven to 350°F.

2. Spread out lamb on a flat surface with inside facing up and trim all visible fat. Spread 2 cloves of minced garlic over

inner surface and sprinkle with rosemary and pepper to taste. Set lamb aside.

3. Heat oil in a large nonstick skillet and sauté onion and remaining garlic over medium heat until lightly browned. Add spinach to skillet, lower heat, and cook for 5 minutes or until spinach is well wilted. Remove skillet from heat, drain off all liquid, then stir in bread crumbs. Let mixture cool slightly.

4. Spread spinach mixture evenly over inside surface of lamb. Roll up lamb, jelly-roll fashion, tucking in ends, and tie well with butcher's string. Place lamb in a shallow roasting pan and roast for about 1½ hours for rare (135°F. on meat thermometer), or 1¾ hours for medium (145°F.). Remove from oven, transfer lamb to a cutting board, and let stand for 10 minutes.

5. While lamb sits, skim off all fat from roasting pan and place pan with remaining juices on stove over medium heat; stir in flour until dissolved. Add water and wine, reduce heat to low, and simmer, stirring constantly, until sauce is thickened and bubbly.

6. Cut lamb into thin slices and arrange on a heated serving platter. Spoon sauce over the sliced lamb and serve.

SERVES 8

APPROXIMATELY 180 MILLIGRAMS SODIUM PER SERVING

◆ ◆ ◆ ◆ ◆

BRAISED LAMB AND GREEN BEANS

▶ ▶

This very flavorful dish originates in the Mideast, where it is traditionally served with steaming rice. Tzatziki (page 28) or a salad of romaine, red onion circles, and orange sections with a vinaigrette dressing would make great side dishes.

1	tablespoon olive oil
2	pounds lean lamb, preferably from the leg, trimmed of all visible fat and cut into 1-inch cubes
2	large onions, finely chopped
2	pounds fresh green beans, trimmed and cut crosswise in half
2	ounces no-salt-added tomato paste
1/2	teaspoon grated nutmeg, or to taste
1/2	teaspoon ground cinnamon, or to taste
1	bay leaf, crumbled
	Freshly ground pepper to taste
	Juice of 1 large lemon

1. Heat oil in a large nonstick stockpot. Add lamb and brown on all sides over high heat. Using a slotted spoon, remove lamb and set aside.

2. Add onions to pot and cook over low heat for 2 minutes or until translucent. Add green beans and cook, stirring often, for an additional 2 minutes.

3. Stir tomato paste into pot, add reserved lamb and all

remaining ingredients. Add enough water to just cover ingredients. Stir to combine, cover, and cook over very low heat, stirring occasionally and adding more water if needed, for 1½ hours or until lamb is tender.

SERVES 8

APPROXIMATELY 84 MILLIGRAMS SODIUM PER SERVING

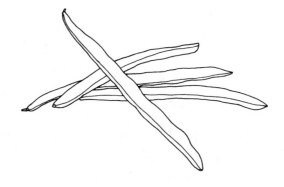

♦ ♦ ♦ ♦ ♦

PORK TENDERLOIN FILLETS STUFFED WITH MUSHROOMS AND HERBS

▶ ▶

The subtle variety of flavors and delightful presentation of this dish belie how simple it is to prepare. The entire dish can be ready in under an hour. Feel free to vary the stuffing ingredients according to your mood. Experiment with sautéed aromatic vegetables or toss in some wine-marinated chunks of fruit.

I usually serve this dish with simple accompaniments such as steamed carrots or green beans.

1	pound pork tenderloin, trimmed of all visible fat
2	teaspoons vegetable oil
1	large shallot, minced
2	large cloves garlic, minced
	Pinch ground allspice
1/2	teaspoon dried thyme
4	tablespoons sherry (not cooking sherry)
3	cups clean, sliced mushrooms
1	tablespoon chopped fresh basil or parsley
	Freshly ground pepper to taste
	Vegetable oil cooking spray
1/4	cup dry red table wine
1/4	cup Low Sodium Beef Stock (page 5)
	Juice of 1 large lemon
	Fresh herb sprigs for garnish

1. Preheat oven to 375°F.
2. Cut tenderloin crosswise into four equal pieces, and

cut each piece in half almost all the way through. Open the cut pieces so they are butterflied and pound each side to a thickness of a little less than 1 inch.

3. Heat 1 teaspoon oil in a large ovenproof skillet. Add shallot, garlic, allspice, and thyme and cook over medium heat until shallot and garlic are soft.

4. Add sherry and mushrooms and cook until mushrooms are tender. Remove mixture with a slotted spoon and coarsely chop. Add basil or parsley and mix well to combine ingredients.

5. Sprinkle the opened sides of the meat with pepper, spread 1/4 of the mushroom mixture over one side of the pork, and flip the still-attached other side of the piece over the top. Secure on a diagonal with a toothpick and set aside. Repeat with the rest of the fillets and filling.

6. Arrange prepared fillets in skillet coated lightly with cooking spray and sear on both sides, turning carefully, over medium-high heat. Cover skillet with foil, transfer to oven, and roast for 25 minutes. Remove foil and roast an additional 10 minutes or until fillets are cooked through and lightly crusted on top. Remove skillet from oven and transfer fillets to a heated platter. Tent with foil and keep warm.

7. Place skillet over medium-high flame and pour in red wine. Bring to a boil and add stock. When mixture returns to a boil, reduce heat to medium-low and simmer for 5 minutes, scraping up any browned particles from the bottom of the skillet. Squeeze the lemon juice into the pan and swirl quickly.

8. Spoon sauce onto warmed plates and lay a cooked fillet in the center of each pool of sauce. Serve garnished with fresh herb sprigs if desired.

SERVES 4

APPROXIMATELY 62 MILLIGRAMS SODIUM PER SERVING

♦ ♦ ♦ ♦ ♦

POLYNESIAN PORK TENDERS

▶ ▶

Don't be afraid to substitute chicken or lean beef strips for the pork and, if you're so inclined, add a dash or two of hot pepper. Accompany with a steaming bowl of cooked brown rice and chopsticks.

1	*pound lean pork tenderloin, trimmed of all visible fat*
2	*teaspoons vegetable oil*
6	*scallions, white and tender greens, chopped*
8	*ounces canned pineapple chunks, juice reserved*
1/4	*cup water*
1	*teaspoon low sodium soy sauce*
1/2	*cup coarsely diced red bell pepper*
1/2	*cup thinly sliced carrots*
1	*cup broccoli florets*
1/2	*cup fresh green beans, cut into 1-inch pieces*
1	*teaspoon freshly grated ginger root*
	Dash hot red pepper flakes, or to taste
1	*tablespoon cornstarch*
1	*teaspoon sugar*
4	*ounces canned, drained water chestnuts*

1. With a sharp knife cut pork tenderloin crosswise into thin slices, then cut into thin strips. Set aside.

2. Heat oil in a large nonstick wok or skillet. Add pork and stir over medium-high heat until it loses its pink color. Using a slotted spoon, remove meat and set aside.

3. Add scallions to skillet and sauté, stirring, for 2 minutes. Add half of the reserved pineapple juice, water, soy sauce, bell pepper, carrots, broccoli, green beans, ginger, and hot pepper if desired. Cover and cook over medium heat for 5 or 6 minutes or until vegetables are just crisp-tender.

4. Combine remaining pineapple juice with cornstarch and sugar, stirring well to blend, and add to vegetable mixture. Cook, stirring constantly, until sauce is slightly thickened.

5. Add water chestnuts, pineapple chunks, and pork and heat through.

SERVES 4

APPROXIMATELY 130 MILLIGRAMS SODIUM PER SERVING

POULTRY

◆ ◆ ◆ ◆ ◆

CHICKEN PICCATA

▶ ▶

One of my favorite dinner-party offerings showcases this fast and easy chicken piccata. I serve this elegant and flavorful dish with tiny sweet peas and new potatoes with rosemary. It is also fabulous with capellini or angel hair pasta tossed with a little olive oil and garlic.

2	*whole boneless, skinless chicken breasts (about 1½ pounds), trimmed of all visible fat and cut in half*
¼	*cup flour*
¼	*teaspoon freshly ground pepper*
2	*teaspoons vegetable oil*
½	*cup Low Sodium Chicken Stock (page 3)*
2	*tablespoons dry vermouth*
2	*tablespoons fresh lemon juice*
4	*thin slices lemon and parsley sprigs for garnish*

1. Pound chicken breast pieces between sheets of plastic wrap to flatten slightly.

2. Dredge chicken in flour combined with pepper and shake off excess.

3. Heat oil in a large nonstick skillet. Add chicken and cook over medium heat for about 4 minutes or until lightly browned. Turn and brown other side for 4 minutes or until cooked through (cooking time will depend on the thickness of the chicken pieces). Transfer chicken to a heated platter and keep warm. Do not wipe skillet.

4. Add stock and vermouth to skillet and bring to a boil. Reduce heat and stir, scraping up browned bits. Add lemon juice and simmer over medium heat, stirring often, for about 2 minutes.

5. Spoon sauce from skillet over chicken, garnish with lemon slices and parsley, and serve immediately.

SERVES 4

APPROXIMATELY 113 MILLIGRAMS SODIUM PER SERVING

◆ ◆ ◆ ◆ ◆

CHICKEN IN CURRIED FRUIT SAUCE

▶ ▶

This unusual recipe with Indian overtones has an absolutely divine aroma and tastes wonderful too. Offer Saffron Rice (page 143) as a side dish.

3	*pound chicken, skinned, trimmed of all visible fat, and cut into 8 serving pieces*
2	*cloves garlic, pressed*
	Freshly ground pepper to taste
2	*teaspoons unsalted butter or margarine, or blend*
2	*teaspoons peanut oil*
1	*medium onion, chopped*
1	*stalk celery, chopped*
1	*tablespoon chopped fresh parsley*
1	*tablespoon curry powder, or more to taste*
1	*cup All-Purpose Tomato Sauce (page 9)*
1/4	*cup water*
1	*large tart apple, preferably Granny Smith, cored and sliced*
1	*ripe but firm banana, sliced*
1/4	*cup golden seedless raisins*
1/4	*cup evaporated low fat milk*

1. Rub chicken pieces with a little of the pressed garlic (about 1/2 clove) and sprinkle with pepper to taste. Heat butter or margarine and oil in a large nonstick skillet. Add chicken and cook over medium heat, turning pieces, until golden. Reduce heat to very low, cover, and cook chicken for 30

minutes or until tender. Using a slotted spoon, remove chicken from skillet and set aside.

2. Add onion and celery to skillet and cook over low heat for 5 minutes. Add parsley, curry powder, tomato sauce, remaining garlic, and water. Stir until ingredients are well blended. Add apple, banana, and raisins, and bring to a simmer. Cover, reduce heat to low, and cook, stirring occasionally, for 10 minutes.

3. Return chicken to skillet, cover, and continue to cook over low heat for 5 minutes or until chicken is heated through. Remove chicken to a heated serving platter.

4. Add evaporated milk to skillet and stir over low heat until well blended. Pour sauce from skillet over chicken and serve.

SERVES 4
APPROXIMATELY 200 MILLIGRAMS SODIUM PER SERVING

♦ ♦ ♦ ♦ ♦

CHICKEN PROVENÇALE

▶ ▶

Garlic, a member of the lily family, is a deceptively innocent-looking bulb consisting of an indefinite number of tightly clustered, demitasse-spoon-shaped cloves individually wrapped in skins of white, mauve, or greenish white, which give no clue whatsoever to the power they pack when peeled!

Garlic is a revered ingredient in many of the dishes of France, Spain, Italy, Greece, Russia, and China. But only Provence—the southern region of France—has created an entire cuisine where garlic is the superstar. This dish is offered as a superb example of that cuisine.

1   tablespoon olive oil
3   pound chicken, skinned, trimmed of all visible
    fat, and cut into serving pieces
1   cup All-Purpose Tomato Sauce (page 9)
1/2 cup dry red or white table wine
1   onion, minced
2   large cloves garlic, finely minced, or more to taste
1   teaspoon thyme
1   bay leaf, crumbled
    Freshly ground pepper to taste

1. Heat oil in a large nonstick skillet and brown chicken pieces on all sides. Remove chicken to a large pot with a tight-fitting lid.

2. Combine tomato sauce with remaining ingredients and pour over chicken.

3. Cook over high heat until sauce starts to simmer. Cover, reduce heat, and simmer gently, stirring occasionally and adding a little water if too much liquid evaporates, for 2 hours or until chicken is tender.

SERVES 4
APPROXIMATELY 171 MILLIGRAMS SODIUM PER SERVING

◆◆◆◆◆

CHICKEN CUTLETS WITH CRANBERRY AND RED ONION SAUCE

▶▶▶▶▶▶▶▶▶▶▶▶▶▶▶▶▶▶▶▶▶▶▶▶▶▶▶

You can put an unexpected spin on turkey-with-cranberry-sauce with this dazzling duo. Serve with kasha or boiled potatoes mashed with low fat milk. Add vegetables or a salad to complete the meal.

2   *whole boneless, skinless chicken breasts (about 1½ pounds), trimmed of all visible fat and cut in half*
2   *tablespoons flour*
½   *teaspoon freshly ground pepper*
1   *tablespoon vegetable oil*
1   *medium red onion, coarsely chopped*
2   *teaspoons sugar*
2   *tablespoons red wine vinegar*
1   *cup fresh cranberries, picked over and rinsed*
    Lemon slices and parsley sprigs for garnish

1. Pound each chicken piece between sheets of wax paper or plastic wrap and flatten to a thickness of about ¼ inch.

2. Dredge chicken in flour combined with pepper and shake off any excess.

3. Heat oil in a large nonstick skillet and cook chicken over medium heat for about 5 minutes on each side or until lightly browned and cooked through.

4. As chicken cooks, combine onion, sugar, and vinegar in a saucepan and stir over medium heat until mixture

becomes syrupy. Reduce heat, stir in cranberries, and simmer over very low heat, stirring often, for about 3 minutes.

5. Remove chicken to a heated serving platter and spoon cranberry mixture over each cutlet. Serve garnished with lemon slices and parsley, if desired.

SERVES 4
APPROXIMATELY 110 MILLIGRAMS SODIUM PER SERVING

◆◆◆◆◆

CHICKEN BAKED IN CREAMY TARRAGON SAUCE

▶▶▶▶▶▶▶▶▶▶▶▶▶▶▶▶▶▶▶▶▶▶▶▶▶▶

Chicken flavored with tarragon originated in France, where a well-salted chicken is generally prepared with a sauce rich in butter and heavy cream. This low sodium version contains far less fat and cholesterol but rivals its French counterpart in taste.

1	tablespoon vegetable oil
2	whole boneless, skinless chicken breasts (about 1½ pounds), trimmed of all visible fat and cut in half
6	scallions, white and tender greens, thinly sliced
12	mushroom caps, wiped clean, thinly sliced
2	teaspoons flour
¾	cup low fat (2%) milk
1	tablespoon chopped fresh tarragon or ½ tablespoon dried
	Freshly ground pepper to taste

1. Preheat oven to 350°F.

2. Heat oil in a large nonstick skillet and sauté chicken over medium heat for 3 minutes on each side or until lightly golden; do not overcook. Transfer chicken to a shallow baking dish.

3. Add scallions and mushrooms to skillet and cook over medium heat for 5 minutes, stirring occasionally.

4. Reduce heat, sprinkle flour over mushrooms and

scallions, and stir until dissolved. Add milk, tarragon, and pepper and stir over low heat until sauce begins to thicken.

5. Spoon ingredients from skillet over chicken breasts and bake for 15 minutes. Serve hot.

SERVES 4

APPROXIMATELY 151 MILLIGRAMS SODIUM PER SERVING

◆ ◆ ◆ ◆ ◆

TURKEY IN PEPPERED POTATO CRUST WITH CHIVE SAUCE

▶ ▶

Turkey is not just for Thanksgiving anymore. Whether it is ground for patties or a loaf, pounded for paillard, poached, roasted, or baked, this once inelegant fowl has been groomed for a wide variety of dishes for every occasion.

In this recipe, the crispy potato crust keeps the turkey moist and juicy. The chive sauce perks everything up, but if you are not a sauce person, eliminate the last four ingredients and 52 milligrams of sodium per serving.

1¹/₂	*pounds boneless, skinless turkey breast, in one piece*
	Freshly ground pepper to taste
1	*pound potatoes, peeled and quartered*
1	*large onion, quartered*
1	*medium green bell pepper, seeded and minced*
1	*tablespoon flour*
2	*large egg whites, slightly beaten*
2	*teaspoons unsalted butter or margarine, or blend*
2	*teaspoons vegetable oil*
¹/₂	*teaspoon dry mustard*
3	*tablespoons light low sodium mayonnaise*
1	*teaspoon fresh lemon juice*
1	*tablespoon chopped fresh chives or 2 teaspoons dried*

1. Cut turkey breast into 4 equal slices. Place slices between sheets of wax paper or plastic wrap and pound, elongating them slightly, into slices approximately 1/2 inch thick. Season to taste with pepper and set aside on a sheet of waxed paper.

2. Grate potatoes and onion in a food processor with a fine grater. Transfer to a mixing bowl and squeeze out as much moisture as possible.

3. Add green pepper, flour, and egg whites to potato-onion mixture and stir until ingredients are well blended.

4. Divide potato mixture into four portions. Pat half of each portion evenly over each turkey slice. Turn turkey and pat remaining potato mixture over other side.

5. Heat butter or margarine and oil in a nonstick skillet large enough to hold all four turkey slices in a single layer. Carefully transfer turkey to skillet and cook over medium to high heat for 5 or 6 minutes on each side or until turkey is cooked through and potato crust is browned. Transfer to a heated serving platter.

6. Stir mustard into mayonnaise until dissolved. Add lemon juice and chives and stir until sauce is well blended. Run a tablespoon of sauce down the center of each turkey slice and serve.

SERVES 4
APPROXIMATELY 195 MILLIGRAMS SODIUM PER SERVING

◆ ◆ ◆ ◆ ◆

BLACKENED TURKEY BREASTS

▶ ▶

On any given night one may observe the hordes of hungry souls who queue up expectantly outside the famous New Orleans eateries that feature blackened fish dishes. The blackening occurs almost as soon as the fish, fresh herbs, and devilishly hot Cajun spices touch down on the well-seasoned cast-iron skillets. And the pleasure of its complex flavors hits at the first mouthful.

Traditionally made with red snapper, catfish, or other fish fillets, my neo-Cajun version works well with chicken or turkey. But be warned: this dish is spicy! You can adjust its temperature by using less—or more—spices. And don't be put off by the seemingly large amount of margarine— most of it remains in the pan.

4	slices boneless turkey breast (about 1½ pounds)
⅓	cup unsalted margarine
1	clove garlic, minced
3	tablespoons dried parsley
1	tablespoon dried oregano
1	tablespoon coarsely ground black pepper
1	teaspoon paprika
1	teaspoon cayenne, or more to taste
1½	tablespoons fresh lemon juice
	Lemon wedges for garnish

1. Refrigerate turkey for at least 2 hours before preparation.

2. Heat margarine in a skillet. Add garlic and stir over medium heat until lightly browned. Remove from heat and stir in all remaining ingredients, except turkey, lemon juice, and lemon wedges. Let mixture cool until margarine starts to harden.

3. Remove turkey from refrigerator and dip into margarine mixture, coating slices well on both sides. Put turkey on a platter, return to refrigerator, and chill for 30 minutes or until margarine has hardened.

4. Heat a large cast-iron skillet over high heat for 2 or 3 minutes. Place turkey, in a single layer, in skillet and cook over high heat for about 5 minutes on each side or until turkey is cooked through.

5. Remove turkey to a heated serving platter and sprinkle with lemon juice. Serve garnished with lemon wedges.

SERVES 4
APPROXIMATELY 115 MILLIGRAMS SODIUM PER SERVING

♦ ♦ ♦ ♦ ♦

TURKEY WALDORF SALAD

▶ ▶

An easy to make, one-dish lunch or light supper for those hot days of summer. For a starter, try the Gazpacho (page 59).

1	*pound cooked white turkey meat*
2	*stalks celery, ends trimmed*
2	*tart apples, preferably McIntosh*
2	*teaspoons fresh lemon juice*
1	*cup seedless white or red grapes*
1/4	*cup coarsely chopped walnuts*
1/3	*cup seedless raisins*
1/2	*cup plus 4 teaspoons minced red onion*
1/2	*teaspoon coarsely ground pepper, or to taste*
3/4	*cup low fat plain yogurt*
1	*small head crisp romaine lettuce, separated into leaves, rinsed, dried, and chilled*

1. Cut turkey into ³/₄-inch cubes. Cut celery stalks crosswise into ¹/₄-inch slices. Cut apples in half, core, cut into 1-inch cubes, and sprinkle with 1 teaspoon lemon juice to prevent discoloring.

2. In a large mixing bowl, combine turkey, celery, and apples with grapes, walnuts, raisins, and ¹/₂ cup red onion. Sprinkle with pepper and toss gently to blend.

3. Combine yogurt and remaining lemon juice and add to turkey mixture. Gently toss again until ingredients are thoroughly blended.

4. Divide romaine leaves into four portions and arrange on individual serving dishes. Place equal portions of salad over romaine and sprinkle a teaspoon of minced red onion over each serving.

SERVES 4
APPROXIMATELY 132 MILLIGRAMS SODIUM PER SERVING

♦ ♦ ♦ ♦ ♦

CORNISH HENS ON
A BED OF ARTICHOKE HEARTS

▶ ▶

The cooking of this dish is accomplished in two parts. First, the hens are prepared. Then, while they bake, you ready the artichoke hearts for cooking. Thus you can cut the total cooking time, finishing both operations almost simultaneously. By the way, I strongly suggest you read through this, or any, recipe before you start to cook. This will give you an idea of what and when items are needed for proper organization and preparation.

2   Cornish game hens, 1¹/₂ pounds each, cleaned and halved (backbones removed)
1   large clove garlic, minced
    Freshly ground pepper to taste
2   tablespoons fresh lemon juice
2   teaspoons vegetable oil
1   stalk celery, diced
¹/₂ cup clean, chopped mushrooms
¹/₂ teaspoon each: dried thyme, tarragon, parsley, and oregano
5   ounces thawed frozen artichoke hearts, coarsely chopped
2   teaspoons cornstarch
2   tablespoons dry white table wine

1. Preheat oven to 400°F.
2. Remove all visible fat from hens. Rub hens inside and

out with half of the minced garlic. Place hens, skin side up, on a rack in a large, shallow baking pan, sprinkle with pepper, and drizzle with 1 tablespoon lemon juice. Roast for 35 to 40 minutes or until hens are cooked.

3. Begin preparation of vegetables about 10 minutes before hens are done. Heat oil in a nonstick skillet, add remaining garlic, celery, and mushrooms, and cook over medium heat, stirring often, for about 2 minutes.

4. Reduce heat and add dried herbs and artichoke hearts. Cover and cook over low heat, stirring occasionally, for 5 minutes.

5. Dissolve cornstarch in wine, add to artichoke mixture, and stir over high heat for 30 seconds or until thickened.

6. Divide artichoke mixture into four equal portions, and spoon onto individual serving dishes or a large heated platter, forming mixture into mounds and placing them so that each hen half will cover a portion. Place 1 hen half, skin side up, over each artichoke mound, drizzle with remaining lemon juice, and serve.

SERVES 4

APPROXIMATELY 145 MILLIGRAMS SODIUM PER SERVING

♦ ♦ ♦ ♦ ♦

ROAST DUCK WITH
SPICED HONEY GLAZE

▶ ▶

While the cholesterol content of duck is very close to that of chicken, duck contains a good deal of fat; however, this method of cooking allows most of it to drain away.

Perfect for that special occasion, this delicious recipe is guaranteed to drive your dinner guests daffy with delight. Steamed pencil-thin asparagus or a chopped fresh leafy green vegetable makes a good adjunct.

4$^1/_2$	pound duck, cleaned and quartered
1	tablespoon grated ginger root
1	large garlic clove, pressed
$^1/_2$	teaspoon turmeric
$^1/_2$	teaspoon ground cumin
$^1/_2$	teaspoon ground cardamom
$^1/_4$	teaspoon cayenne, or to taste
1	tablespoon fresh lemon juice
$^1/_3$	cup honey
$^3/_4$	cup apple juice

1. Preheat oven to 350°F.

2. Using a small sharp knife, gently lift skin of duck and cut away as much fat as you can reach, then pierce skin in several places.

3. Combine ginger, garlic, turmeric, cumin, cardamom, cayenne, and lemon juice. Rub inside and outside of duck pieces with mixture. Place duck, skin side up, on a rack in a

roasting pan. Roast for 45 minutes, piercing skin every 10 minutes. Remove from oven and drain off all accumulated fat from roasting pan. Raise oven temperature to 425°F.

4. Combine honey and apple juice and brush ¼ of mixture over duck. Return duck to oven and roast for an additional 30 minutes, basting with honey–apple juice mixture every 10 minutes, or until duck is fully cooked and well glazed.

SERVES 4
APPROXIMATELY 112 MILLIGRAMS SODIUM PER SERVING

FISH
and
SHELLFISH

◆ ◆ ◆ ◆ ◆

SCROD WITH MUSTARD CRUST

▶ ▶

Cod is a family of fish containing a number of familiar white-fleshed American relatives, including Atlantic and Pacific cod, haddock, hake, pollock, and scrod.

Scrod is actually Atlantic cod that comes to the market weighing 1½ to 2½ pounds. But whatever its alias, this firm lean fish beloved by East and West coasters alike can be poached, baked, sautéed, braised, or used in soups and stews.

Serve this version with baked sweet potato, squash, or Green Rice (page 148).

1½	pounds scrod fillets
	Vegetable oil cooking spray
1	tablespoon unsalted butter or margarine, softened
1	tablespoon dry mustard, or to taste
	Dry white table wine
	Paprika to taste
	Lemon slices and parsley sprigs for garnish

1. Preheat broiler.

2. In a single layer, place fillets side by side in a shallow baking dish coated with cooking spray and set aside.

3. Combine butter or margarine with mustard into a thick paste. Slowly add wine and stir until consistency is similar to a smooth prepared mustard.

4. Brush mustard-wine mixture evenly over fish fillets, and sprinkle lightly with paprika. Place about 3 inches from

heat source and broil, without turning, for 7 or 8 minutes or until fish flakes when pierced with a fork.

5. Transfer fish to a heated serving platter, garnish with lemon slices and parsley sprigs if desired, and serve.

SERVES 4
APPROXIMATELY 95 MILLIGRAMS SODIUM PER SERVING

◆ ◆ ◆ ◆ ◆

FILLET OF SOLE
WITH SHALLOT SAUCE

▶ ▶

Because sole cooks quickly, prepare this dish just before serving. Use the stove timer, a stopwatch, or set your alarm clock—but don't overcook the fish or it will be dry and tasteless. Sole should be moist and tender.

This delicate fish, so easily overwhelmed by heavier sauces, shines through in a light blend of shallots and white wine. Sweet and Sour Leeks (page 159) or Creamy Broccoli Puree (page 169) would make a delightful accompaniment. For dessert? Treat everybody to vanilla ice milk smothered in fresh strawberry sauce.

1¹/₄	*pounds sole fillets*
1	*tablespoon vegetable oil*
3	*medium shallots, minced*
	Freshly ground pepper to taste
1	*tablespoon fresh lemon juice*
¹/₂	*cup dry white table wine*
1	*teaspoon cornstarch*
¹/₄	*cup water*
	Thin lemon slices and parsley sprigs for garnish

1. Heat oil in a large nonstick skillet. Add fish and sauté over medium heat for about 3 minutes on each side or until fish flakes when pierced with a fork. Transfer fish to a heated serving platter and keep warm.

2. Add shallots, pepper, and lemon juice to skillet and

stir over medium heat for 5 minutes. Add wine and bring to a boil. Dissolve cornstarch in water and add to skillet. Reduce heat and stir until sauce thickens.

3. Spoon sauce over fish, garnish with lemon slices and parsley if desired, and serve.

SERVES 4
APPROXIMATELY 118 MILLIGRAMS SODIUM PER SERVING

◆ ◆ ◆ ◆ ◆

GINGER-GLAZED TUNA STEAKS

▶ ▶

This recipe is simple to make but there are two vital keys to its success: use the freshest tuna you can get your hands on and avoid overcooking. Calculate cooking time for tuna steaks at 8 minutes per inch, regardless of cooking method, adding 4 minutes per inch if they're submerged in sauce (rather than brushed with it as in this preparation).

Serve with crispy bean sprouts and cilantro drizzled with a bit of sesame oil and rice wine vinegar. Heat some sake, the flavorful Japanese rice wine, and try it with this dinner.

4	*tuna steaks, about 6 ounces each, 1 1/2 inches thick*
	Vegetable oil cooking spray
2	*teaspoons vegetable oil*
1	*clove garlic, finely minced*
1 1/2	*tablespoons freshly grated ginger root*
2	*teaspoons sugar*
1/2	*cup plus 2 tablespoons water*
2	*teaspoons cornstarch*

1. Preheat broiler.

2. Arrange tuna steaks in a single layer on a broiling pan or shallow roasting pan lightly coated with cooking spray and set aside.

3. Heat oil in a nonstick skillet. Add garlic and ginger root and stir over medium heat for 2 minutes. Add sugar and 1/2 cup water and stir until sugar is dissolved.

4. Blend cornstarch with 2 tablespoons water and add to ginger mixture. Stir over medium heat until thickened.

5. Brush half the ginger sauce over top of tuna steaks. Place tuna about 3 inches from heat source and broil for 5 minutes. Remove from oven, turn fish over, and brush with remaining sauce. Broil an additional 5 minutes or to desired degree of doneness.

SERVES 4

APPROXIMATELY 61 MILLIGRAMS SODIUM PER SERVING

♦ ♦ ♦ ♦ ♦

SALMON AND RED ONIONS
BRAISED IN RED WINE

▶ ▶

Salmon is probably the most universally admired fish, whether it is the smoked variety of Ireland, Scotland, and Nova Scotia (long off-limits for us salt-smart folks), or the more sodium-conscious poached, broiled, and grilled salmon now so readily available in restaurants throughout the country.

This simple creation of salmon braised in a red wine–based liquid shows how far we've progressed from that old saw—that only white wine with fish is appropriate.

Complement with rice, noodles, or potatoes.

1	*tablespoon vegetable oil*
2	*medium red onions, thinly sliced*
³/₄	*cup dry red table wine*
1¹/₂	*pounds salmon fillet, preferably in one piece*
¹/₂	*cup Low Sodium Chicken Stock (page 3)*
¹/₄	*cup minced fresh parsley*
1	*teaspoon dried thyme*
	Freshly ground pepper to taste
	Fresh parsley sprigs for garnish

1. Heat oil in a large nonstick skillet. Add onions and stir gently over medium heat for 3 minutes. Add ¹/₂ cup of red wine to skillet and bring to a boil. Cover, reduce heat to low, and simmer gently for 5 minutes or until onions are softened.

2. Stir parsley, thyme, and pepper to taste into skillet.

Spread onions evenly and place salmon fillet over onions. Pour remaining wine and stock over salmon. Bring to a boil, then reduce heat, cover, and cook, basting salmon frequently with wine, for about 10 minutes or until salmon flakes easily when pierced with a fork.

3. Remove salmon to a heated serving platter. Using a slotted spoon, remove onions and arrange around salmon. Return skillet to heat and cook over high heat until liquid is reduced to about ¼ cup. Spoon liquid from skillet over salmon, garnish with parsley sprigs if desired, and serve.

SERVES 4

APPROXIMATELY 83 MILLIGRAMS SODIUM PER SERVING

HALIBUT WITH FRESH PESTO

This dish, made with a lemony pesto sauce, embodies the glory of summer no matter what the season. Make a big batch of pesto in summertime, when basil is at its freshest and most flavorful, and freeze it for use all year long.

Try this with Herb-Sautéed Summer Squash (page 165) and fresh ripe tomatoes for a sumptuous Mediterranean-inspired meal.

1½   pounds halibut fillets
      Vegetable oil cooking spray
2   tablespoons fresh lemon juice
1½   cups packed fresh basil leaves
½   cup packed fresh parsley leaves
3   tablespoons pine nuts
2   cloves garlic, chopped
1   tablespoon olive oil

1. Preheat broiler.

2. Place halibut in a single layer on a broiling pan or shallow baking pan coated with cooking spray. Spray fish lightly with oil and sprinkle with 1 tablespoon lemon juice. Broil about 3 inches from heat source for 8 minutes, without turning, or until fish flakes when pierced with a fork.

3. While fish broils, combine basil, parsley, pine nuts, garlic, and remaining lemon juice in food processor and process for 10 seconds or until smoothly pureed. With processor running, add oil in a slow, steady stream.

4. Transfer fish to a heated serving platter and top with sauce, or serve sauce on the side.

SERVES **4**

APPROXIMATELY **90** MILLIGRAMS SODIUM PER SERVING

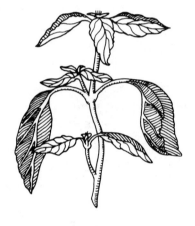

FLOUNDER STUFFED WITH SALMON IN DILLED WINE SAUCE

▶ ▶

Even my friend Liz (who has been known to broil a simple steak to ashes) has received culinary kudos with this surprisingly simple, elegant-looking dish. And so will you. Don't let the number of ingredients turn you off—it's not difficult to prepare and it's well worth trying.

Serve with steamed baby carrots and zucchini. And for dessert, try poached spiced pears in wine.

4	flounder fillets, about 5 ounces each
	Freshly ground pepper to taste
2	tablespoons fresh lemon juice
4	ounces cooked salmon fillet, skinned and flaked
1	ounce pimientos, minced
2	tablespoons minced scallions
1	egg, beaten, or frozen egg substitute equal to 1 egg
1	tablespoon cornstarch
	Vegetable oil cooking spray
4	teaspoons unsalted butter or margarine
1/2	cup dry white table wine
1	tablespoon minced fresh dill or 2 teaspoons dried

1. Preheat oven to 350°F.

2. Sprinkle both sides of flounder with pepper and 1 tablespoon of the lemon juice. Set aside.

3. Combine salmon with remaining lemon juice, pimientos, scallions, egg, and 1/2 tablespoon cornstarch. Mash until ingredients are well blended.

4. Spread ¼ of salmon mixture over one side of flounder fillet. Roll up fillet, jelly-roll fashion, and secure with a
toothpick. Repeat with remaining three fillets and salmon
mixture.

5. Place fish rolls side by side in a small baking pan or
ovenproof casserole lightly coated with cooking spray. Dot
each roll with 1 teaspoon butter or margarine and pour wine
over all. Bake for about 20 minutes or until fish is opaque and
flakes easily when gently pierced with a fork.

6. Remove fish rolls from baking pan, place on a heated
serving platter, and keep warm.

7. Place baking pan on stove top over low heat. Add
remaining cornstarch and dill and stir until sauce thickens
and starts to bubble. Spoon sauce over fish rolls and serve.

SERVES 4

APPROXIMATELY 148 MILLIGRAMS SODIUM PER SERVING

◆ ◆ ◆ ◆ ◆

BROILED CATFISH CAJUN STYLE

▶ ▶

Wild catfish thrive from the Great Lakes south to Virginia and west to Mexico. Although the wild breed is still considered a delicacy in New Orleans, catfish are now farmed and cultivated in more than 40 states. The farmed variety are sweet tasting, lean, and white, while the wild variety has a slight earthy flavor some consider muddy tasting.

Serve this spicy dish with Sweet Potatoes Pureed with Garlic and Rosemary (page 175) and stewed tomatoes with okra, or with pimiento rice and steamed chopped kale.

1	teaspoon chili powder
1/2	teaspoon ground cumin
1/4	teaspoon cayenne, or to taste
2	teaspoons minced garlic
1	tablespoon olive oil
1 1/2	pounds catfish fillets
	Vegetable oil cooking spray
2	tablespoons chopped fresh cilantro or parsley

1. Combine chili powder with cumin, cayenne, and garlic. Add olive oil and stir into a paste. Brush paste over both sides of catfish and refrigerate for about 1 hour.

2. Preheat broiler.

3. Place catfish in one layer in a shallow baking pan

coated with cooking spray. Broil fish about 3 inches from heat source for 5 minutes on each side.

4. Transfer fish to a heated serving platter, sprinkle with cilantro or parsley, and serve.

SERVES 4

APPROXIMATELY 115 MILLIGRAMS SODIUM PER SERVING

◆ ◆ ◆ ◆ ◆

CHILLED POACHED SEA BASS WITH ONION CUCUMBER DILL SAUCE

▶ ▶

While water is certainly an adequate poaching liquid, a simple *court bouillon* of water and wine blended with herbs, spices, and aromatic vegetables really does make a difference. One of the nicest toppings for any poached fish is my Onion Cucumber Dill Sauce, which can be put together very quickly.

Boiled small new potatoes with skin, halved and lightly dosed with margarine and paprika, and a salad of bitter greens (arugula, radicchio, chicory, Belgian endive) make good accompaniments for this dish.

1	cup dry white table wine
1	cup water
1	small onion, sliced
1	stalk celery, sliced
1	small carrot, sliced
3	sprigs parsley
8	whole peppercorns
1	bay leaf
1	teaspoon dried thyme
1¹/₄	pounds sea bass fillets
³/₄	cup low fat plain yogurt
¹/₄	cup light sour cream
¹/₂	small onion, grated
1	medium cucumber, peeled, seeded, and coarsely chopped

2   tablespoons minced fresh dill weed or 1
    tablespoon dried
1   teaspoon fresh lemon juice
1   teaspoon dry mustard
    Dill sprigs and thin lemon slices for garnish

1. Make the court bouillon by combining wine, water, sliced onion, celery, carrot, parsley, peppercorns, bay leaf, and thyme in a saucepan. Bring to a boil, then reduce heat to low, cover, and simmer gently for 30 minutes.

2. Strain the court bouillon (discard solids or use for another purpose) and transfer liquid to a fish poacher or steamer, or to a large deep skillet. Add fish, cover, and steam or simmer for 10 to 12 minutes or until fish flakes easily when pierced with a fork. Carefully remove fish to a serving platter and cool to room temperature. Cover fish and refrigerate for 1 hour.

3. Prepare sauce by combining yogurt and sour cream with grated onion, cucumber, dill, lemon juice, and mustard. Stir until ingredients are thoroughly blended. Chill sauce until fish is ready to serve.

4. Arrange fish on a serving platter, garnish with dill and lemon slices, and serve accompanied by sauce.

SERVES 4
APPROXIMATELY 140 MILLIGRAMS SODIUM PER SERVING

◆ ◆ ◆ ◆ ◆

BAKED SWORDFISH
IN GARLICKY CITRUS SAUCE

▶ ▶

This party pleaser is simple to prepare and a delight for maven and amateur alike.

Serve with steamed green snow peas, Tabbouleh (page 155), or your favorite pasta dish.

	Vegetable oil cooking spray
1/4	*cup minced fresh parsley*
	Freshly ground pepper to taste
1/2	*teaspoon ground cardamom*
2	*garlic cloves, pressed*
1	*tablespoon olive oil*
4	*swordfish steaks, about 5 ounces each*
1	*tablespoon fresh lemon juice*
	Juice of 1 large orange
1	*teaspoon orange zest*
	Thin slices of lemon or orange for
	garnish

1. Preheat oven to 350°F. Coat a shallow baking dish with cooking spray and set aside.

2. Blend together parsley, pepper, cardamom, garlic, and oil. Spread half of the mixture over one side of fish, turn fish over, and spread with remaining mixture.

3. Combine lemon and orange juices with orange zest and pour over fish steaks.

4. Place fish in a single layer in prepared baking dish.

Bake 8 minutes on each side or until fish flakes easily when pierced with a fork. Transfer to a heated platter, garnish with lemon or orange slices if desired, and serve.

SERVES 4

APPROXIMATELY 133 MILLIGRAMS SODIUM PER SERVING

◆ ◆ ◆ ◆ ◆

STIR-FRIED LEMON SHRIMP
WITH FRESH VEGETABLES

▶ ▶

Stir-frying is extremely popular today. And why not? It's a quick, healthy, and flavorful way to cook, and you can create scores of dishes using just about any combination of meat, poultry, seafood, or vegetables.

Unfortunately, stir-fried recipes usually call for soy sauce, which is off-limits in the prescribed quantities. I have found lemon to be an appealing alternative, and my Lemon Garlic Vinaigrette is a wonderful addition to this and other stir-fry combinations.

Just remember stir-fries are cooked in minutes, so have all your ingredients ready to throw into the wok before you begin.

1	pound large shrimp, shelled and deveined
³/₄	cup Lemon Garlic Vinaigrette (page 15)
2	teaspoons vegetable oil
2	teaspoons sesame oil
1	clove garlic, minced
2	outer stalks bok choy (Chinese cabbage), thinly sliced
1	red bell pepper, seeded and thinly sliced
6	scallions, white and tender greens, cut diagonally into 1-inch slices
³/₄	cup sliced water chestnuts
¹/₄	pound fresh snow pea pods
	Hot red pepper flakes to taste

1   tablespoon cornstarch
2   tablespoons cold water
1   teaspoon fresh lemon juice

1. In a small mixing bowl, toss shrimp with vinaigrette and refrigerate for 15 minutes.

2. Heat vegetable and sesame oils in a nonstick wok or large skillet. Add garlic, bok choy, and bell pepper. Stir over medium heat for 4 minutes. Add scallions, water chestnuts, snow peas, and red pepper flakes if desired. Lower heat slightly and stir for an additional 4 minutes.

3. Add shrimp and vinaigrette to wok or skillet and stir over medium heat for about 4 minutes or until shrimp is cooked.

4. Dissolve cornstarch in water and lemon juice and add to skillet. Raise heat and stir for 1 minute or until sauce thickens. Serve hot.

SERVES 4
APPROXIMATELY 200 MILLIGRAMS SODIUM PER SERVING

◆ ◆ ◆ ◆ ◆

SCALLOPS WITH
GARLIC AND WHITE WINE

▶ ▶

To paraphrase Will Rogers: I never met a scallop I didn't like! Sweet, delicate, and tender, they need barely any garnish or preparation at all.

This is the kind of dish you want to serve when your best pals, or the best palates you know, are coming for dinner. I even serve it for myself as an extravagant reward for any job well done.

Accompany with braised leeks dressed in their own cooking liquid and Saffron Rice (page 143).

1   *pound large scallops*
1   *tablespoon unsalted butter*
2   *garlic cloves, finely minced*
1/4   *cup minced shallots*
1/2   *cup dry white table wine*
1   *tablespoon minced fresh parsley*
     Paprika to taste

1. Rinse scallops, pat dry, and set aside.
2. Heat butter in a large nonstick skillet. Cook garlic and shallots over low heat, stirring often, for 5 minutes.
3. Raise heat. When butter starts to foam, add scallops and cook over high heat for 2 minutes. Turn scallops, lower heat, and cook for an additional 2 minutes or until scallops are creamy white. Using a slotted spoon, transfer scallops to a heated serving platter and keep warm.

4. Add wine and parsley to skillet and stir over high heat until wine comes to a boil. Remove from heat and spoon wine sauce over scallops. Sprinkle with paprika to taste and serve immediately.

SERVES 4
APPROXIMATELY 187 MILLIGRAMS SODIUM PER SERVING

PASTA
and
GRAINS

◆ ◆ ◆ ◆ ◆

FETTUCCINE WITH SCALLOPS, SUN-DRIED TOMATOES, AND PEPPERS

▶ ▶

Children love pasta. Just watch them as they happily devour it—clasping the squirmy strands, pushing them into their mouths, and blissfully slurping away until hands, face, and clothing are coated with sauce. We, on the other hand, twirl our forks, or use forks with spoons (*"Gauche!"* cry the elite) to help us shovel the stuff. The Asians have always used chopsticks for this purpose, their heads lowered to meet the noodles at bowl level—a neat way to eat noodles.

To this day, however, I can't help but succumb to some primordial Jungian urge to use my fingers to scarf down leftover pasta with childlike glee, my sauce-stained face a dead giveaway. In any case, it's hard to imagine leftovers after you serve this delicious fettuccine.

6   *no-salt-added sun-dried tomato halves* (*not oil packed*)
1   *cup boiling water*
³/₄   *pound uncooked fettuccine*
1   *tablespoon olive oil*
2   *cloves garlic, minced*
1   *stalk celery, minced*
1   *medium green bell pepper, seeded and cut into thin strips*
1   *medium yellow or red bell pepper, seeded and cut into thin strips*

1   tablespoon fresh oregano or 1 teaspoon dried
    Freshly ground pepper to taste
$^1/_2$ cup dry white table wine
$^3/_4$ pound small scallops or large scallops quartered,
    rinsed, and drained
1   tablespoon minced fresh parsley

1. Soak sun-dried tomatoes in boiling water for 5 minutes to soften. Drain tomatoes and set aside.

2. Slide pasta into boiling, unsalted water.

3. While fettuccine cooks, heat oil in a large skillet. Add garlic and celery and cook over low heat, stirring, for 1 minute.

4. When tomatoes are cool enough to handle, cut into thin strips and add to skillet along with bell peppers. Stir over medium heat for 2 minutes. Sprinkle with oregano and freshly ground pepper, if desired.

5. Raise heat, add wine, and bring to a boil. Reduce heat, add scallops, and simmer gently, stirring often, for about 4 minutes or until scallops are just cooked. Remove from heat, cover, and keep warm until pasta is cooked.

6. When pasta is al dente, drain and transfer to a heated serving bowl or platter, top with scallop mixture, sprinkle with parsley, and serve immediately.

SERVES 4
APPROXIMATELY 164 MILLIGRAMS SODIUM PER SERVING

◆ ◆ ◆ ◆

LINGUINE WITH
EGGPLANT AND FRESH MINT

▶ ▶

I first tasted this unusual combination of mint and tender braised eggplant as an appetizer in a quaint Italian restaurant in upstate New York. Recurring longings finally induced me to recreate the taste, and this pasta dish is the result of that quest.

For best results use fresh mint and get small, young eggplants, which are far less bitter than the larger ones and do not require salting and draining.

1	tablespoon olive oil
1	small onion, diced
2	cloves garlic, minced
2	small eggplants (about 6 ounces each), trimmed and cut into 1-inch cubes
1	16-ounce can no-salt-added plum tomatoes, drained and coarsely chopped
1/2	teaspoon hot red pepper flakes, or to taste
	Juice of one large lemon
1	tablespoon chopped fresh oregano or 1 teaspoon dried
1	tablespoon chopped fresh thyme or 1 teaspoon dried
3/4	pound uncooked linguine
3	tablespoons coarsely chopped fresh mint

1. Heat oil in large, deep nonstick skillet or saucepan. Add onion and cook over medium heat, stirring often, until wilted. Add garlic and cook for 2 minutes.

2. Add eggplant and cook, shaking pan occasionally, until eggplant begins to brown. Raise heat and add tomatoes, hot pepper, lemon juice, and oregano and thyme if you are using dried herbs. Bring to a boil, then reduce heat, cover, and simmer gently for 15 minutes.

3. While sauce simmers, cook linguine in unsalted water until al dente.

4. Drain pasta and add to eggplant mixture along with mint and other fresh herbs if you are using them. Toss gently to coat linguine, transfer to heated pasta bowls, and serve immediately.

SERVES 4

APPROXIMATELY 30 MILLIGRAMS SODIUM PER SERVING

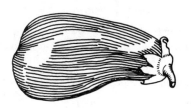

◆ ◆ ◆ ◆ ◆

SMALL SHELLS
WITH CHILI SAUCE

▶ ▶

When I was growing up, an extremely popular advertising campaign grabbed the country by its funny bone. It showed Giuseppe Q. Public with an animated, if distressed, face saying, "*Mama mia!* That's a speecy-spicy meatball!" The commercial went on to show our poor actor/protagonist being asked to do it again. Giuseppe/actor dutifully eats another meatball. Then another, and another, until the off-camera voice of the director, finally satisfied with the take, says the blessed words, "Cut. Print it!" Meanwhile, our poor actor, now obviously suffering from acute stomach pain, sighs in relief after pouring himself a glass of sparkling antacid. This dish won't send you running for the fizz, but nonetheless, it *is* spicy.

I like this recipe because the spiciness doesn't overwhelm the wonderfully complex flavors. Serve with a simple salad of romaine and chopped watercress and string beans, and pass a pitcher of ice tea with cranberry juice as a refresher.

³/₄	*pound very lean ground beef*
1	*large onion, chopped*
2	*large cloves garlic, chopped*
1	*tablespoon chili powder*
¹/₄	*teaspoon cayenne, or to taste*
¹/₂	*teaspoon cumin*
1	*28-ounce can no-salt-added plum tomatoes, chopped, with juice*

1   medium green bell pepper, cored, seeded, and
    diced
1   fresh jalapeño pepper, seeded and minced
    (optional)
1   teaspoon dried oregano
½   teaspoon ground coriander
1   pound uncooked small pasta shells

1. Scatter beef in a large nonstick skillet or pot. Turn on heat and raise slowly to medium. Stir beef with a wooden spoon as it begins to cook, breaking up any clumps. Continue cooking until meat begins to brown. Remove beef with a slotted spoon and set aside.

2. Drain off all fat but do not wipe skillet. Add onion to skillet and cook over medium heat, stirring often, until onion is wilted. Add garlic and cook until garlic just begins to turn golden. Add chili powder, cayenne, and cumin, stirring to dissolve.

3. Raise heat, add tomatoes, bell and jalapeño peppers, oregano, coriander, and reserved beef, and stir to combine ingredients. Cover, reduce heat, and simmer gently for about 20 minutes.

4. When sauce is nearly done, cook pasta in unsalted water until al dente.

5. Drain pasta, transfer to a heated serving bowl, and toss with a few tablespoons of the sauce. Serve remaining sauce separately.

SERVES 6

APPROXIMATELY 85 MILLIGRAMS SODIUM PER SERVING

PENNE WITH MIXED SWEET PEPPERS, ONIONS, AND HERBS

Pasta is the perfect last-minute supper, and this dish goes from cupboard to table in under 30 minutes. The most time-consuming part is the seeding and dicing of the bell peppers. But the confetti colors make it look—and taste—like a labor of love.

It will feel like New Year's Eve when you present this colorful dish. So celebrate! Serve with arugula salad dressed in your best olive oil, balsamic vinegar with minced garlic, and a couple of grinds from the peppermill, crusty bread, and, of course, dry red or white wine. Fruit sorbet topped with fresh mint leaves and freshly brewed decaf espresso with a touch of Sambucca or other licorice-flavored liqueur are a perfect way to end the evening.

1   *tablespoon olive oil*
1   *small red onion, sliced into rings and quartered*
3   *medium bell peppers (any combination of red, orange, yellow, or purple), seeded and diced*
3   *medium cloves garlic, finely minced*
1   *16-ounce can no-salt-added plum tomatoes, coarsely chopped, with juice*
3/4 *pound uncooked penne (quill-shaped pasta)*
1   *tablespoon fresh oregano or 1/2 tablespoon dried*
2   *teaspoons chopped fresh thyme or summer savory or 1 teaspoon dried*
    Freshly ground pepper to taste

1. Heat oil in large, deep nonstick skillet. Sauté onion and peppers over medium-low heat, stirring frequently, until onion is wilted. Add garlic and cook until garlic shows flecks of gold. Raise heat and add tomatoes (mixture will splatter at first). Simmer for 2 minutes, then reduce heat, cover partially, and simmer gently for 10 minutes.

2. While sauce simmers, slide penne into boiling, un-salted water.

3. When pasta is cooked al dente, drain well, add to tomato and pepper mixture in skillet, and sprinkle with herbs and pepper to taste. Toss to coat, transfer to heated pasta bowls, and serve.

SERVES 4

APPROXIMATELY 29 MILLIGRAMS SODIUM PER SERVING

◆ ◆ ◆ ◆ ◆

CHILLED ROTINI AND CHICKEN SALAD IN CREAMY TOMATO SAUCE

▶ ▶

This main-dish pasta salad requires no more accompaniment than a good glass of wine to make a satisfying light lunch or supper.

4	cups cooked rotini (spiral) pasta, chilled
1½	cups diced cooked white meat chicken
4	scallions, with tops, sliced
1	stalk celery, diced
12	cherry tomatoes, cut in half
¼	cup chopped fresh cilantro
¼	cup low fat ricotta cheese
2	tablespoons light sour cream
¾	cup All-Purpose Tomato Sauce (page 9) or canned low sodium tomato sauce, chilled
½	teaspoon cumin seeds
½	teaspoon fennel seeds
	Freshly ground pepper to taste
	12 to 16 crisp romaine lettuce leaves

1. In a large mixing bowl, combine pasta with chicken, scallions, celery, tomatoes, and cilantro. Toss gently to blend ingredients and set aside.

2. Combine ricotta cheese with sour cream, tomato sauce, cumin and fennel seeds, and pepper to taste. Stir until smooth and well blended.

3. Pour ricotta mixture over pasta and chicken mixture and toss lightly to combine and coat ingredients.

4. Divide lettuce among 4 serving dishes and top with equal portions of pasta salad.

SERVES 4

APPROXIMATELY 87 MILLIGRAMS SODIUM PER SERVING

MACARONI SALAD
WITH VEGETABLES IN
YOGURT MUSTARD SAUCE

▶ ▶

The best thing about tonight's turkey is usually tomorrow's leftovers. I feel the same way about roasted chicken, meat loaf, and roast beef. This cold macaroni salad is just the dish to serve with those longed-for leave-behinds. It's also terrific to take along on a picnic, to the beach, or even to the office.

3	*ounces drained marinated artichoke hearts*
1	*stalk celery*
6	*small radishes*
1	*small red onion*
1	*carrot*
1	*small red or green bell pepper, seeded*
2	*tablespoons chopped fresh parsley or basil*
3	*cups cooked elbow macaroni, chilled*
1	*tablespoon dry mustard*
2	*tablespoons dry white table wine*
1/2	*teaspoon cumin seeds*
1	*cup low fat plain yogurt*
	Freshly ground pepper to taste

1. Cut artichoke hearts into large pieces and finely dice all remaining vegetables.

2. In a large mixing bowl, combine vegetables and parsley with macaroni and toss lightly to blend.

---

3. Mix mustard and wine until mustard is dissolved. Add mustard mixture and cumin seeds to yogurt and stir until ingredients are well blended. Season to taste with pepper and stir again.

4. Spoon dressing onto macaroni and vegetables and toss until ingredients are well coated.

SERVES 4

APPROXIMATELY 63 MILLIGRAMS SODIUM PER SERVING

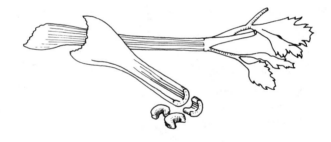

SAFFRON RICE

A perfect complement to any fish or shellfish, this rice also makes a good base for steamed mixed vegetables, stews, or any curry dish.

    2   teaspoons vegetable oil
    2   large shallots, minced
    1   stalk celery, chopped
    1   medium yellow bell pepper, seeded and diced
   ¹/₄ teaspoon crumbled saffron threads, or to taste
    1   cup uncooked white rice
   2¹/₂ cups Low Sodium Chicken Stock (page 3)
        Freshly ground pepper to taste

1. Heat oil in a large nonstick pot. Add shallots, celery, and bell pepper and stir over medium heat for 3 minutes.

2. Add saffron and rice to pot and stir briefly to coat rice. Add chicken stock and season to taste with pepper. Bring to a boil, cover, reduce heat, and simmer gently for about 30 minutes or until rice is tender.

SERVES 4
APPROXIMATELY 28 MILLIGRAMS SODIUM PER SERVING

RICE WITH FRESH FENNEL AND PIGNOLIAS

▶ ▶

Fennel, a licorice-flavored bulb long used in Mediterranean cooking, is quickly gaining popularity in this country. This recipe combines fennel with rice and pignolia nuts and makes a perfect accompaniment to fish or roast poultry.

I've also made this dish using wild rice in place of the white (adding two tablespoons of currants) and found that the nutty flavor of the wild rice works exceptionally well with the fennel.

$^1/_2$	*pound fennel bulb, outer stalks and tops removed*
1	*tablespoon vegetable oil*
4	*scallions, white and tender greens, sliced*
1	*teaspoon dried thyme*
	Freshly ground pepper to taste
1	*cup uncooked white rice*
3	*cups Low Sodium Chicken Stock (page 3)*
3	*tablespoons pignolia nuts*

1. Rinse fennel well in cold water, dice, and set aside.

2. Heat oil in a large saucepan. Add fennel and scallions and cook over low heat, stirring occasionally, for 5 minutes. Stir in thyme and pepper to taste.

3. Add rice to fennel mixture and stir briefly to coat

---

grains. Add stock and bring to a boil. Cover, reduce heat, and simmer gently for about 40 minutes or until rice is cooked.

4. Stir in pignolia nuts and serve.

SERVES **4**

APPROXIMATELY **75** MILLIGRAMS SODIUM PER SERVING

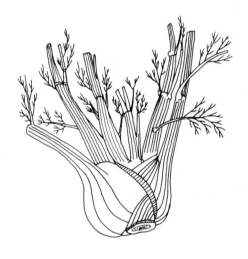

◆ ◆ ◆ ◆ ◆

SHRIMP RISOTTO

▶ ▶

For purists, Italian Arborio rice is an essential ingredient for risotto. Plump and oval-grained, Arborio has the capacity to absorb more stock and flavor from liquid than ordinary rice. It is both creamy and chewy, leading to the great controversy among aficionados as to whether a risotto should be eaten with a fork or a spoon.

Here is a fabulous risotto that's sure to stir up the controversy and fire up any genuine culinary sensibility. Serve with crisp-steamed mixed vegetables and a salad of sliced tomatoes. Complete the meal with a compote of stewed fruits topped with a dollop of light sour cream or plain yogurt.

1	cup water
1/2	pound shrimp in shell
3	cups Low Sodium Chicken Stock (page 3)
1/4	cup minced fresh parsley
	Freshly ground pepper to taste
1	tablespoon olive oil
1	medium onion, minced
1/4	cup minced red bell pepper
1	cup uncooked Arborio rice (available at Italian markets and larger supermarkets)

1. Bring water to a boil in a large saucepan. Add shrimp, reduce heat, and simmer gently for about 3 minutes or until shrimp is just cooked. Using a slotted spoon, remove shrimp

and cool. When cool enough to handle, shell, devein, and coarsely chop shrimp and set aside.

2. Add stock, parsley, and ground pepper to water in saucepan and bring to a simmer over very low heat.

3. Heat oil in a large, deep nonstick skillet. Add onion and red pepper and cook over low heat, stirring often, for 5 minutes or until onion is translucent. Add rice to skillet and stir briefly to coat grains.

4. Gradually add simmering stock mixture to skillet, 1/4 cup at a time, and stir over medium heat until liquid is absorbed. Continue adding stock in 1/4-cup measures, stirring constantly, until rice has absorbed all the liquid and is just tender.

5. Add shrimp to rice and stir over low heat until shrimp is heated through. Serve immediately.

SERVES 4
APPROXIMATELY 107 MILLIGRAMS SODIUM PER SERVING

♦ ♦ ♦ ♦ ♦

GREEN RICE

▶ ▶

A good companion for all fish, seafood, and poultry dishes, this rice has the gumption to stand on its own merits as well. Serve with a salad of cucumbers and yogurt with fresh mint and a dessert of fresh strawberries marinated in lemon juice and sugar for a dinner so good your friends will be green with envy.

1	tablespoon unsalted butter or margarine, or blend
6	scallions, with tops, minced
1	medium green bell pepper, seeded and diced
1	cup uncooked white rice
3	cups water
1	cup chopped fresh parsley
2	cups chopped fresh spinach
1	teaspoon dried thyme
$^{1}/_{2}$	teaspoon dried tarragon
	Freshly ground pepper to taste
$^{3}/_{4}$	cup frozen and thawed green peas

1. Heat butter or margarine in a large saucepan. Add scallions and bell pepper and cook over low heat, stirring often, for 5 minutes.

2. Add rice and stir over medium-low heat for 1 minute. Stir in water and bring to a boil. Reduce heat to very low, cover, and cook for 15 minutes.

3. Add parsley, spinach, thyme, tarragon, and ground

pepper to taste. Cover and cook for an additional 15 minutes or until rice is just tender.

4. Stir in peas, raise heat slightly, and simmer for about 3 minutes or until peas are cooked.

SERVES 4
APPROXIMATELY 68 MILLIGRAMS SODIUM PER SERVING

PAELLA SALAD NOUVEAU

▶ ▶

When served on a bed of crisp fresh greens, this unusual and spectacular salad contains all the elements of an entire meal. Although my low sodium adaptation of the Spanish classic does require time and attention, the results are definitely worth the effort.

Offer warm crusty bread and, if desired, a dry white wine.

2	cups water
1/4	cup dry white table wine
1 1/2	cups Low Sodium Chicken Stock (page 3)
1/2	boneless, skinless chicken breast (about 6 ounces), trimmed of all visible fat
24	large shrimp, shelled and deveined
1/4	pound sole or flounder fillets
2	dozen fresh small clams, scrubbed
1	tablespoon olive oil
1	onion, minced
2	cloves garlic, minced
1/4	teaspoon crumbled saffron threads, or to taste
1/4	teaspoon hot red pepper flakes, or to taste
1	cup uncooked long-grain white rice
2	tablespoons chopped fresh parsley
3/4	cup frozen and thawed green peas
2	ripe plum tomatoes, seeded and chopped
1	stalk celery, chopped
1	medium green bell pepper, seeded and diced

2   ounces canned pimientos, drained and
    diced
6   scallions, with tops, thinly sliced
¹/₄ cup pitted, sliced black olives
2   tablespoons fresh lemon juice
    Garnish: Shredded crisp greens (about 12 cups),
    1 ounce pimiento cut into thin strips, and 2
    lemons, each cut into 6 wedges

1. Bring water, wine, and stock to a boil in a large saucepan. Add chicken, reduce heat, and simmer until tender. Using a slotted spoon, remove chicken from water and set chicken aside to cool.

2. Add shrimp, sole or flounder, and clams to liquid in saucepan and bring to a boil. Reduce heat slightly and simmer for 5 to 10 minutes or until fish is cooked. With a slotted spoon remove fish and shellfish from saucepan as they cook, discarding any clams that have not opened, and set aside to cool. Keep cooking liquid simmering over very low heat.

3. Heat oil in a large, deep skillet or pot. Add onion and garlic and stir over medium heat until lightly browned. Reduce heat to low, sprinkle saffron and pepper flakes over onion, add rice, and stir until rice is coated. Add hot cooking liquid and parsley to rice. Stir gently, cover, and simmer over low heat for 15 minutes.

4. Add peas to rice and continue to simmer for an additional 15 minutes or until rice is tender. Transfer rice to a large mixing bowl and cool.

5. While rice cools, cut chicken into cubes, flake sole or flounder, and remove clams from their shells.

6. When rice has cooled, add chicken, fish, and shellfish, tomatoes, celery, green pepper, pimientos, scallions, and

olives. Sprinkle with lemon juice and toss gently until ingredients are combined. Cover and refrigerate for at least 2 hours.

7. On a large platter or individual serving dishes, arrange salad over greens, top with pimiento strips, and surround with lemon wedges.

SERVES **6**

APPROXIMATELY **190** MILLIGRAMS SODIUM PER SERVING

◆ ◆ ◆ ◆ ◆

CHILLED RICE PRIMAVERA

▶ ▶

This vegetarian dish makes life easier when I have friends over for a casual party. A perfect component in a buffet setting, this rice and vegetable salad goes on a table along with other delectables that might include a roasted chicken studded with garlic and rosemary (which I dramatically slice onto an awaiting platter) and a large bowl of green salad.

$^3/_4$	cup uncooked long-grain white rice
1	cup water
$1^1/_2$	cups Low Sodium Vegetable Stock (page 7)
1	teaspoon unsalted butter or margarine, or blend
1	clove garlic, minced
4	shallots, minced
1	carrot, cut diagonally into $^1/_4$-inch slices
1	ripe plum tomato, chopped
1	small zucchini, cut diagonally into $^1/_4$-inch slices
6	stalks asparagus, trimmed and cut diagonally into $^1/_2$-inch slices
1	cup broccoli florets
3	tablespoons balsamic vinegar
1	tablespoon olive oil
	Freshly ground pepper to taste
1	tablespoon chopped fresh parsley
4	scallions, white and tender greens, thinly sliced

1. Cook rice in water and 1 cup of stock until tender. Set aside to cool.

2. Heat butter or margarine in a large nonstick skillet. Add garlic and shallots and cook over low heat, stirring, for 1 minute.

3. Stir remaining stock into skillet. Add carrot and cook over low heat for 5 minutes. Raise heat to medium, add tomato, zucchini, asparagus, and broccoli, and simmer for 3 to 5 minutes or until vegetables are crisp-tender. Drain vegetables, transfer to a mixing bowl, and set mixture aside to cool.

4. Prepare dressing by combining vinegar with oil, pepper, and parsley.

5. Combine cooled rice and vegetables, sprinkle with scallions, add dressing, and toss gently to blend ingredients. Serve chilled or at room temperature.

SERVES 4

APPROXIMATELY 27 MILLIGRAMS SODIUM PER SERVING

◆ ◆ ◆ ◆ ◆

TABBOULEH

▶ ▶

This cool and tasty salad has its origins in the Mideast, where it is generally prepared with copious amounts of oil. My light version makes a good side dish for roast lamb or poultry. It also makes a delectable light lunch for two accompanied by Tzatziki (page 28) and hot pita.

1	cup fine bulgur (about 4 ounces)
2	cups water
¹/₄	cup minced scallions
¹/₂	cup minced red onion
1	ripe tomato, coarsely chopped
¹/₂	cup chopped fresh parsley
3	tablespoons chopped fresh mint or 1 tablespoon dried
1	tablespoon olive oil
2	tablespoons fresh lemon juice
	Freshly ground pepper to taste

1. Soak bulgur in water for about 1 hour to reconstitute. Drain and squeeze out as much moisture as possible, then spread out bulgur on an absorbent towel to dry further.

2. Transfer bulgur to large mixing bowl. Add remaining ingredients and toss until thoroughly blended. Refrigerate for at least 1 hour before serving.

SERVES 4 AS A SIDE DISH
APPROXIMATELY 15 MILLIGRAMS SODIUM PER SERVING

VEGETABLES

◆ ◆ ◆ ◆ ◆

SWEET AND SOUR LEEKS

▶ ▶

It would be virtually impossible for me to imagine a week going by without cooking with the vegetable that is so ubiquitous in France it is called the poor man's asparagus. From soups and stews to sauces and salads, the leek's flavor blends with almost everything.

Leeks, the national emblem of Wales, are a distinguished member of the onion/lily family. They look like huge, overgrown scallions made husky by pumping iron.

Nearly every cook I know, professional or otherwise, has at least one onion handy in the vegetable bin, but few pay homage to the singular and venerable leek. If you have never experimented with leeks, this piquant preparation is a grand introduction.

4   *medium leeks, white and tender greens*
1   *tablespoon peanut oil*
3   *cloves garlic, minced*
2   *teaspoons sugar*
2   *tablespoons fresh lemon juice*

1. Cut leeks in half lengthwise and rinse well under running water, separating leaves gently to remove any hidden soil. Cut leeks in half lengthwise again and set aside.

2. Heat oil in a large nonstick skillet. Add garlic and sugar and cook over medium heat, stirring constantly, until sugar starts to caramelize.

3. Add leeks and stir to coat them with garlic-sugar

mixture. Sprinkle mixture with lemon juice, cover, reduce heat to very low, and cook until leeks are tender.

SERVES 4

APPROXIMATELY 21 MILLIGRAMS SODIUM PER SERVING

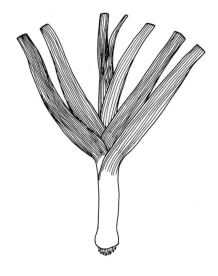

◆ ◆ ◆ ◆ ◆

CABBAGE BAKED
IN YOGURT SAUCE

▶ ▶

Even the most daring chefs shy away from serving the hearty fare offered in this robust recipe in their restaurants. Long considered peasant fare, it is only in the more comfortable confines of chefs' home kitchens that dishes of this nature make their appearance. That's a shame because these chefs are not sharing with the public the savory, homey dishes they treasure the most.

This cabbage dish deserves an audience beyond the sodium-smart denizens of the range who, by necessity or culinary curiosity, have the gumption to experiment with a wide variety of tastes and textures.

2   teaspoons peanut oil
1   large onion, thinly sliced
1   small head green cabbage (about 1 pound), cored and shredded
2   medium potatoes, peeled and thinly sliced
1   teaspoon dried oregano
     Vegetable oil cooking spray
$^1/_2$ cup dry white table wine
2   teaspoons cornstarch
1   teaspoon mild or hot paprika, or to taste
     Freshly ground pepper to taste
$^3/_4$ cup low fat plain yogurt
3   tablespoons minced fresh parsley
1   tablespoon grated Parmesan cheese

1. Heat oil in a large nonstick skillet. Add onion and cook over low heat, stirring occasionally, for about 5 minutes or until onion is soft.

2. Add cabbage and potatoes to skillet in alternating layers and sprinkle with oregano. Cover, reduce heat to very low, and simmer gently for 40 minutes, stirring occasionally.

3. Preheat oven to 350°F. Coat a baking dish or oven-proof casserole lightly with cooking spray and set aside.

4. Drain and discard liquid from vegetables in skillet. Add wine, raise heat to medium, and cook, uncovered, for 5 minutes.

5. Using a large spatula, transfer contents of skillet to prepared baking dish or casserole. Pour in any liquid from skillet.

6. Stir cornstarch, paprika, and pepper into yogurt and add to vegetables. Toss gently to blend and sprinkle with parsley and grated Parmesan cheese. Bake for 20 minutes. Serve immediately.

SERVES 4

APPROXIMATELY 80 MILLIGRAMS SODIUM PER SERVING

◆◆◆◆◆

ACORN SQUASH BAKED
WITH CRANBERRIES AND WALNUTS

▶▶▶▶▶▶▶▶▶▶▶▶▶▶▶▶▶▶▶▶▶▶▶▶▶▶

Acorn squash is one of the sturdy, full-flavored vegetables of autumn. This recipe makes a wonderful side dish for almost any meat or poultry entrée. The fragrant and delicious cranberries and walnuts lend a piquant contrast of flavors.

2	acorn squash (about 1 pound each)
4	tablespoons plus ¹/₂ cup apple juice
¹/₄	cup dry red table wine
2	tablespoons brown sugar or honey
1	cup fresh cranberries, picked over and rinsed
2	tablespoons chopped walnuts

1. Preheat oven to 350°F.

2. Cut squash in half crosswise and scoop out and discard seeds. Cut a thin slice from the bottom skin side of each squash half to make it stand level. Place squash halves, cut side up, in a shallow baking pan. Spoon 1 tablespoon apple juice into each cavity. Add water to pan to a depth of ¹/₂ inch and bake squash for 10 minutes.

3. While squash bakes, combine wine and remaining apple juice with sugar or honey in a small saucepan and bring to a boil, stirring. Reduce heat slightly, add cranberries, and simmer for 5 minutes. Remove from heat and stir in walnuts.

4. After squash has baked for 10 minutes, remove from oven and spoon cranberry mixture into cavities. Add a little

more water to baking pan if needed, return squash to oven, and bake for an additional 15 minutes or until squash is tender when pierced with a fork. Serve hot.

SERVES 4
APPROXIMATELY 9 MILLIGRAMS SODIUM PER SERVING

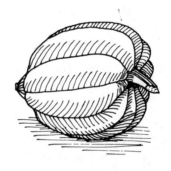

HERB-SAUTÉED SUMMER SQUASH

▶ ▶

One of the great virtues of zucchini is that just about anyone can grow one. Herein also lies the problem: nobody can grow just one! So fecund is the zucchini that even my amateur gardener friends bemoan its overpopulation in their once varied vegetable patches.

So, at summer's end it's not unusual to find zucchini at one's doorstep—in a host of guises: zucchini pies, breads, and cakes are popular offerings, as are the endless zucchini pickles, preserves, and, yes, whole, unadulterated zucchini.

One of the more welcome methods of using and enjoying this stud of the garden is in conjunction with its less prolific cousin, the yellow or crookneck squash.

Simply sautéed with shallots and tomato, redolent of herbs, this dish metamorphoses into one of aromatic grace.

2   small yellow summer squash
2   small zucchini
1   tablespoon olive oil
2   medium shallots, chopped
1   teaspoon chopped fresh marjoram or $1/2$ teaspoon dried
1   teaspoon chopped fresh thyme or $1/2$ teaspoon dried
1   teaspoon chopped fresh oregano or $1/2$ teaspoon dried

1   teaspoon chopped fresh basil or ½ teaspoon dried
    Freshly ground pepper to taste
2   ripe plum tomatoes, chopped
1   tablespoon grated Parmesan cheese

1. Trim ends and cut yellow squash and zucchini diagonally into ¼-inch slices.

2. Heat oil in a large nonstick skillet. Add yellow squash, zucchini, shallots, herbs, and pepper. Stir over medium heat for 2 minutes.

3. Add tomatoes, cover, reduce heat to low, and simmer gently for an additional 2 to 3 minutes or until vegetables are just tender.

4. Transfer contents of skillet to a heated serving dish and sprinkle with grated Parmesan cheese.

SERVES 4

APPROXIMATELY 32 MILLIGRAMS SODIUM PER SERVING

◆ ◆ ◆ ◆ ◆

HONEY-GLAZED CARROTS

▶ ▶

Glazing is basically the application of a coating that gives foods a smooth, glossy surface. Ingredients used for glazing include butter, reduced meat juices, reduced stocks, gelatin, simple sugar syrups, corn syrup, and honey. Widely used in France and to a lesser extent in this country, glazing not only improves the appearance of foods but also enhances flavors.

Honey-glazed carrots are a wonderful counterpoint to any simply prepared meat or poultry dish. They also go surprisingly well with curried lamb, beef, or poultry.

> 1   *pound carrots, cut diagonally into ¹/₄-inch slices*
> 1¹/₂ *tablespoons unsalted butter or margarine, or blend*
> 1   *cup water*
> 1   *teaspoon fresh lemon juice*
> 2   *tablespoons honey*
>   *Freshly ground pepper to taste*
> 2   *teaspoons toasted sesame or sunflower seeds (optional)*

1. Combine all ingredients, except sesame or sunflower seeds, in a nonstick skillet and bring to a boil. Cover, reduce heat, and simmer gently for about 8 minutes or until carrots are just tender.

2. Remove cover, raise heat to medium-high, and shake

skillet until most of the liquid has evaporated and carrots are glazed.

3. Transfer contents of skillet to a heated serving dish and sprinkle with sesame or sunflower seeds if desired.

SERVES 4

APPROXIMATELY 37 MILLIGRAMS SODIUM PER SERVING

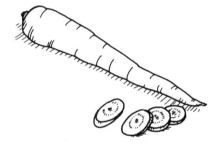

CREAMY BROCCOLI PUREE

▶ ▶

Broccoli is a veritable medicine cabinet of nutrition. The head-of-household of the cruciferous family of vegetables (which may have cancer-preventing properties), it is low in calories and sodium. One serving provides 90 percent of our daily requirement of vitamin A, 200 percent of vitamin C, 10 percent of thiamine, 10 percent of phosphorus, and 8 percent of iron. It is also rich in potassium and fiber.

When crisp-steamed, broccoli has a bright, delicious flavor I find hard to resist; in cahoots with sour cream, sautéed onion, and rosemary, it becomes sheer poetry.

Vegetable oil cooking spray
1   *pound broccoli, tough stalks removed*
2   *teaspoons unsalted butter or margarine, or blend*
1   *small onion, chopped*
1 1/2   *teaspoons dried rosemary*
Freshly ground pepper to taste
3   *tablespoons light sour cream*
3   *tablespoons no-salt-added low fat cottage cheese*

1. Preheat oven to 375°F. Coat a baking dish or oven-proof casserole with cooking spray and set aside.

2. Rinse broccoli and cut into florets. Steam until broccoli is just tender. Drain well and transfer to a food processor.

3. Heat butter or margarine in a nonstick skillet and sauté onion for 3 or 4 minutes or until soft. Stir in rosemary and pepper to taste.

4. Add contents of skillet to food processor and blend for 5 seconds or until coarsely pureed. Add sour cream and cottage cheese and process for another 5 seconds or until just blended.

5. Transfer broccoli mixture to prepared baking dish or casserole and bake for 10 minutes or until bubbly. Serve hot.

SERVES 4

APPROXIMATELY 32 MILLIGRAMS SODIUM PER SERVING

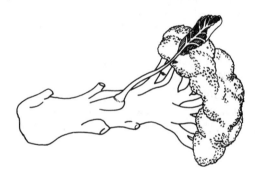

◆◆◆◆◆

CAULIFLOWER WITH LEMON AND MINT

▶▶▶▶▶▶▶▶▶▶▶▶▶▶▶▶▶▶▶▶▶▶▶▶▶▶

Cauliflower, another member of the cruciferous family of vegetables, is low in calories, provides healthy doses of vitamin C and potassium, and is rich in fiber. That it is so flavorful is an added bonus.

In this recipe, the flavors of mint and lemon bring vibrancy to the cauliflower and play extremely well with meat, fish, or poultry.

1 *head cauliflower (about 1 pound), trimmed*
2 *tablespoons fresh lemon juice*
1 *tablespoon olive oil*
    Freshly ground pepper to taste
1/4 *cup coarsely chopped fresh mint or 2 tablespoons dried*
    Mint leaves for garnish

1. In a large saucepan, boil cauliflower in unsalted water to which 1/2 tablespoon lemon juice has been added, for 10 minutes or until just tender. Drain well and break cauliflower into florets.

2. Heat oil in a large nonstick skillet and stir in the remaining lemon juice. Add cauliflower florets and sprinkle with pepper to taste. Cook over low heat, stirring to coat all surfaces of cauliflower with oil-lemon mixture, for 1 minute.

3. Sprinkle chopped mint over the cauliflower in skillet. Cover, reduce heat to very low, and simmer for 5 minutes.

---

4. Transfer contents of skillet to a heated serving platter, garnish with mint leaves, and serve hot.

SERVES 4
APPROXIMATELY 10 MILLIGRAMS SODIUM PER SERVING

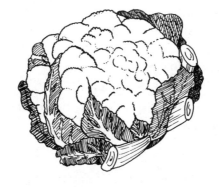

◆ ◆ ◆ ◆ ◆

TOFU-STUFFED EGGPLANT
WITH SPICY TOMATO SAUCE

▶ ▶

This dish is a favorite among my rigid, health-conscious vegetarian friends. Served with brown rice, millet, barley, or kasha, this Oriental spin on an old favorite makes a filling, delicious meal.

2	*eggplants (about 1 pound each)*
	Vegetable oil cooking spray
1	*tablespoon olive oil*
1	*large onion, chopped*
2	*large cloves garlic, finely minced*
1	*small carrot, finely diced*
1	*cup clean, sliced mushrooms (about ¼ pound)*
¾	*pound firm tofu, drained and crumbled*
¼	*cup chopped fresh parsley or cilantro*
1	*ripe tomato, chopped*
	Freshly ground pepper to taste
1	*cup plus 4 tablespoons Spicy Tomato Sauce (page 11)*

1. Preheat oven to 350°F.

2. Cut eggplants in half lengthwise. Leaving shells intact, carefully scoop out pulp to within ¼ inch of shells. Transfer shells, cut side up, to a shallow baking pan lightly coated with cooking spray, and set aside.

3. Dice eggplant pulp into ¼-inch squares and set aside.

4. Heat oil in a large nonstick skillet. Add onion, garlic, and carrot and cook over medium heat, stirring often, for 3 minutes.

5. Add mushrooms and eggplant pulp and stir. Cover, reduce heat to low, and cook, stirring occasionally, for about 5 minutes.

6. Add tofu, parsley, tomato, ground pepper, and 1 cup of tomato sauce. Stir to blend ingredients, then cover and cook for an additional 5 minutes, stirring occasionally.

7. Spoon mixture from skillet into the four eggplant shells, then spoon 1 tablespoon of the remaining tomato sauce over each stuffed shell. Bake for 30 minutes. Serve immediately.

SERVES 4

APPROXIMATELY 52 MILLIGRAMS SODIUM PER SERVING

◆ ◆ ◆ ◆ ◆

SWEET POTATOES PUREED
WITH GARLIC AND ROSEMARY

▶ ▶

The juxtaposition of rosemary and garlic with sweet potatoes produces an unusually savory alternative to the more traditional sugared sweet potato purees associated with the festive holiday celebrations of Thanksgiving, Christmas, and Rosh Hashanah (Jewish New Year). But you need not wait for a special occasion—this delicious dish is superb served with just about any grilled or braised meat or fowl.

	Vegetable oil cooking spray
4	medium sweet potatoes
2	tablespoons unsalted butter or margarine, or blend
3	cloves garlic, coarsely chopped
1	medium onion, chopped
2	teaspoons dried rosemary
	Freshly ground pepper to taste
2	tablespoons finely minced scallions or parsley

1. Preheat oven to 350°F. Coat an ovenproof serving dish or casserole with cooking spray and set aside.

2. Pierce skin of potatoes in several places and bake for 45 minutes or until tender.

3. While potatoes bake, heat butter or margarine in a nonstick skillet. Add garlic and onion and cook over medium heat, stirring occasionally, for about 8 minutes or until well

browned but not burned. Stir in rosemary and ground pepper to taste. Remove from heat and let cool slightly.

4. When potatoes are done, scoop out and transfer pulp to a food processor. Add contents of skillet and process until coarsely pureed (if necessary, do this in several batches). Transfer mixture to prepared casserole.

5. Bake for 10 minutes or until bubbling. Remove from oven, sprinkle top with minced scallions or parsley, and serve hot.

SERVES 4
APPROXIMATELY 21 MILLIGRAMS SODIUM PER SERVING

◆ ◆ ◆ ◆ ◆

WHITE BEANS AND VEGETABLES IN HERBED TOMATO SAUCE

▶ ▶

I had to include my adaptation of this northern Italian specialty because it's extremely low in sodium for a dish that's so abundant in flavor.

1	tablespoon olive oil
1	medium onion, diced
1	stalk celery, diced
1	carrot, diced
3	cloves garlic, minced
1	cup fresh green beans, cut diagonally into 1-inch pieces
1/2	cup dry white table wine
1	teaspoon dried basil
1/2	teaspoon dried rosemary
1/2	teaspoon dried oregano
2	tablespoons minced fresh Italian parsley
4	ripe plum tomatoes, coarsely chopped
1	cup All-Purpose Tomato Sauce (page 9)
	Hot red pepper flakes to taste
2 1/2	cups cooked (not canned) small white beans
1	tablespoon grated Parmesan cheese

1. Preheat oven to 350°F.

2. Heat oil in a large nonstick skillet. Add onion, celery, and carrot, and cook over medium heat for 2 minutes, stirring occasionally.

3. Add garlic and cook for 30 seconds, then reduce heat to low, add green beans, wine, basil, rosemary, oregano, and parsley. Simmer gently, stirring often, for 2 minutes.

4. Add tomatoes, tomato sauce, hot pepper flakes if desired, and white beans to skillet. Stir gently, bring to a boil, and remove from heat.

5. Transfer contents of skillet to an ovenproof casserole that can be used for serving, and sprinkle top with grated Parmesan cheese. Bake for 20 minutes. Serve immediately.

SERVES 4 GENEROUSLY

APPROXIMATELY 57 MILLIGRAMS SODIUM PER SERVING

◆ ◆ ◆ ◆ ◆

STUFFED SWEET PEPPERS

▶ ▶

The color combination of the ingredients in this recipe makes an extremely attractive presentation and the mushrooms add a meaty taste without the fat of meat.

2	teaspoons vegetable oil
1	stalk celery, diced
1/2	pound fresh mushrooms, wiped clean, trimmed, and thinly sliced
3/4	cup corn kernels, fresh or frozen and thawed
1 1/2	teaspoons fennel seeds
1/2	teaspoon ground turmeric
1	cup cooked rice
	Freshly ground pepper to taste
4	large red, yellow, or orange bell peppers, or mixture
1/2	cup low fat ricotta cheese

1. Preheat oven to 350°F.

2. Heat oil in a large nonstick skillet. Add celery and mushrooms and cook over low heat, stirring often, for 5 minutes. Add corn and cook for an additional 5 minutes.

3. Raise heat to medium, add remaining ingredients, except bell peppers and cheese, and cook, shaking pan occasionally, until most of the liquid has evaporated. Remove from heat and cool slightly.

4. Cut tops off peppers and carefully remove seeds. (If peppers are wobbly, you may have to trim the bottoms

slightly so that they stand up, but be careful not to cut all the way through.)

5. Combine ricotta with the cooled skillet mixture and mix to blend well. Fill the cavities of the peppers with ricotta mixture.

6. Stand the stuffed peppers upright in a small baking dish, add water to a depth of ¹/₂ inch, cover with foil, and bake for 30 minutes. Remove foil and bake for an additional 15 minutes. Serve hot.

SERVES 4

APPROXIMATELY 38 MILLIGRAMS SODIUM PER SERVING

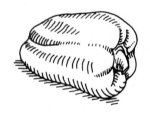

◆ ◆ ◆ ◆ ◆

POTATO AND ASPARAGUS SALAD
WITH CREAMY HERB DRESSING

▶ ▶

We're so used to thinking of "potato salad" as a fixed culinary phrase that it comes as a surprise when we invert the words into "salad of potatoes." Then it occurs to us that we are free to do a host of things besides loading on the mayonnaise, celery, and hard-cooked eggs.

In this recipe, boiled, peeled potatoes make the perfect foil for fresh asparagus cooked just long enough to turn a vivid green. The salad is enhanced still further by the presence of crimson-cast sun-dried tomatoes, regally dressed with a yogurt-herb mixture.

1	*pound potatoes, peeled and cut into 1¹/₂-inch cubes*
¹/₂	*pound asparagus, trimmed of tough stalk ends and cut into 1-inch pieces*
4	*no-salt-added sun-dried tomato halves (not oil packed), softened in boiling water*
4	*scallions with tops, thinly sliced*
¹/₄	*cup low fat plain yogurt*
¹/₄	*cup no-salt-added low fat cottage cheese*
1	*tablespoon fresh lemon juice*
1	*teaspoon dried tarragon*
1	*teaspoon dried thyme*
1	*tablespoon minced fresh parsley or 2 teaspoons dried*
	Freshly ground pepper to taste

1. Cook potatoes in unsalted water until tender. Drain and set aside to cool in a large mixing bowl.

2. Steam asparagus until just crisp-tender. Drain and add to mixing bowl with potatoes to cool.

3. Drain and dice sun-dried tomatoes and add along with scallions to potatoes and asparagus.

4. Combine yogurt and cottage cheese with remaining ingredients, stirring to blend thoroughly. Add yogurt mixture to cooled potato mixture and toss gently until all ingredients are combined. Serve at room temperature or cover and refrigerate for 1 hour before serving.

SERVES 4

APPROXIMATELY 30 MILLIGRAMS SODIUM PER SERVING

RED CABBAGE AND APPLE SLAW WITH POPPY-SEED DRESSING

I adore this slaw because the ingredients provide contrasting sweet and sour tastes and a variety of textures.

1½ tablespoons light low sodium mayonnaise
2 teaspoons sugar
3 tablespoons red wine vinegar
½ small red onion, quartered
1½ tablespoons vegetable oil
2 teaspoons poppy seeds
3 cups shredded red cabbage
1 large tart apple, preferably McIntosh or Granny Smith, peeled, halved, cored, and thinly sliced
¼ cup seedless raisins
2 teaspoons fresh lemon juice

1. To prepare dressing, combine mayonnaise, sugar, vinegar, and onion in a food processor. Process until onion is finely minced. With motor running, add oil in a slow, steady stream. Transfer dressing to a small mixing bowl and stir in poppy seeds.

2. In a large mixing bowl, toss cabbage with apples, raisins, and lemon juice. Pour dressing over cabbage mixture and toss again until ingredients are well blended and coated with dressing. Chill or serve at room temperature.

SERVES 4

APPROXIMATELY 33 MILLIGRAMS SODIUM PER SERVING

♦ ♦ ♦ ♦ ♦

ROOT VEGETABLE PIE

▶ ▶

This autumn/winter side dish complements any simple roast or broiled meat, poultry, or fish. It's also popular at hot buffets. And I have served it as an entrée at a vegetarian dinner for four, preceded by a hearty soup and accompanied by a large salad.

> Vegetable oil cooking spray
> 1 medium carrot, cut crosswise in half
> 1 medium onion, quartered
> 2 medium potatoes, quartered
> 2 medium turnips or 1 small rutabaga (about 1 pound), trimmed, peeled, and quartered
> Thawed frozen egg substitute equal to 2 eggs
> Freshly ground pepper to taste
> 1/2 teaspoon dried rosemary
> 1/4 teaspoon dried tarragon
> 3 tablespoons all-purpose flour
> Bread crumbs made from 1 slice dry whole wheat bread
> 2 tablespoons minced fresh parsley
> 1 tablespoon grated Parmesan cheese

1. Preheat oven to 350°F. Coat a large pie plate or baking dish, preferably glass, with cooking spray and set aside.

2. Using the large grating attachment of a food processor, grate carrot, onion, potatoes, and turnips or

rutabaga in separate batches. Transfer to a large mixing bowl.

3. Squeeze out as much excess moisture from grated vegetables as possible. Add egg substitute, pepper, rosemary, tarragon, and flour and mix thoroughly.

4. Spoon mixture into prepared pie plate or baking dish, spreading and smoothing top with back of spoon. Combine remaining ingredients and sprinkle over vegetables. Cover loosely with foil and bake for 20 minutes.

5. Remove foil and bake for an additional 20 minutes or until top is crisp and browned and vegetables are cooked through.

6. Remove from oven, let stand for 1 minute, then cut into six wedges and serve.

SERVES 6
APPROXIMATELY 101 MILLIGRAMS SODIUM PER SERVING

◆ ◆ ◆ ◆ ◆

CURRIED VEGETABLES

▶ ▶

On a recent occasion I prepared a simple but good roasted chicken for my family and neighbors. It was an impromptu meal, put together at the last moment, and I used foods that were available at that time—an improvised and user-friendly meal indeed. My chicken demanded a cooking time of 45 minutes and I got it started in the oven before getting on to the curried vegetables. Once the bird started to brown, I peeled the potatoes, cut them into cubes, and proceeded from there.

All your foods can be timed to be ready for the table at more or less the same moment, with just a little planning, even when your meal's the result of a spur-of-the-moment inspiration.

1   *medium potato, peeled and cut into 1¹/₂-inch cubes*
1   *large carrot, cut into ¹/₂-inch slices*
6   *ounces green beans, trimmed and cut into 1-inch lengths*
2   *teaspoons peanut oil*
4   *scallions, with tops, coarsely chopped*
2   *teaspoons minced ginger root*
1   *tablespoon curry powder, or to taste*
1   *teaspoon ground cardamom*
     Pinch cayenne (optional)
¹/₂ *cup Low Sodium Chicken Stock (page 3)*
2   *ripe plum tomatoes, chopped*
1   *cup corn kernels, fresh or frozen and thawed*

---

1. Boil potatoes in unsalted water for 5 minutes. Add carrot, reduce heat to low, and simmer gently for 4 minutes. Add green beans and continue to simmer for an additional 2 minutes or until vegetables are barely tender. Remove from heat, drain, and set vegetables aside.

2. Heat oil in a large nonstick skillet. Add scallions and ginger and cook over low heat, stirring often, for 3 minutes. Add curry powder, cardamom, cayenne, and chicken stock and stir over medium heat for 2 minutes.

3. Add reserved vegetables, chopped tomatoes, and corn, stir gently, and cook over medium heat for about 5 minutes or until all vegetables are tender. Serve immediately or keep warm in heated oven.

SERVES 4
APPROXIMATELY 20 MILLIGRAMS SODIUM PER SERVING

DESSERTS

♦♦♦♦♦

BASIC DESSERT CREPES

▶▶▶▶▶▶▶▶▶▶▶▶▶▶▶▶▶▶▶▶▶▶▶▶▶

For a simple but delicious dessert, offer these crepes warm, spread with preserves or brushed lightly with melted unsalted butter, folded into quarters and sprinkled with confectioners' sugar, or topped with yogurt and almost any fresh or frozen fruit.

These versatile crepes can be made in advance and refrigerated or frozen (layer them between sheets of waxed paper) until ready to use.

If you're cutting back on your cholesterol intake and want to eliminate the eggs, use a frozen egg substitute equivalent to two whole eggs.

> $^3/_4$ cup all-purpose flour
> 2 tablespoons confectioners' sugar, or to taste
> 2 eggs
> $^2/_3$ cup low fat (2%) milk
> $^1/_3$ cup water
> $^1/_4$ teaspoon vanilla extract or grated lemon rind (optional)
> Vegetable oil cooking spray

1. Sift together flour and sugar into a mixing bowl.

2. In a separate bowl, combine eggs with milk and water, and add vanilla extract or lemon rind if desired. Beat mixture until well blended.

3. Form a well in center of flour-sugar mixture and pour in egg-milk mixture. Beat lightly to blend ingredients (don't

worry about lumps in the batter, they'll disappear during cooking).

4. Heat a 7- or 8-inch nonstick crepe pan or skillet and lightly coat the inside surface with cooking spray. Add 2 to 2½ tablespoons of batter (this will depend on the size of the pan). Gently tip the pan so that batter spreads evenly in a thin layer over the bottom surface and about ⅛ inch up on sides. (If batter is too thick, stir in a tablespoon or more water.) Cook over medium heat for 30 seconds or until crepe is lightly browned. Turn and brown other side. Remove crepe to a platter. Repeat until all batter has been used (there should be enough to make 12 crepes).

MAKES ABOUT 12 CREPES
APPROXIMATELY 19 MILLIGRAMS SODIUM PER CREPE

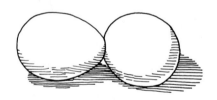

PLUM AND ALMOND CREPES

Impress your friends, your family, your boss, and your-self with these unusual and scrumptious fruit and nut crepes.

  1   *tablespoon unsalted butter or margarine, or blend*

  3   *plums, preferably Damson, halved, pitted, and sliced*

  ¼ *cup golden seedless raisins*

  2   *tablespoons firmly packed brown sugar*

  2   *teaspoons fresh lemon juice*

  ½ *teaspoon ground cinnamon, or to taste*

  2   *teaspoons Amaretto liqueur (optional)*

  2   *tablespoons chopped almonds*

  1   *recipe Basic Dessert Crepes (page 191)*

  8   *teaspoons light sour cream*

1. Melt butter or margarine in a saucepan. Add plums, raisins, sugar, lemon juice, cinnamon, and Amaretto if desired. Cover and simmer over very low heat, stirring occasionally, for 10 to 15 minutes or until plums are well cooked. Remove from heat, stir in almonds, and set aside to cool for 5 minutes.

2. While plums simmer, prepare crepes, using a 10- to 12-inch diameter skillet and using 3 to 3½ tablespoons of batter per crepe (there should be enough batter for 8 large crepes). As they cook, remove crepes to a heated platter and keep warm.

3. Spoon a dollop of plum mixture in the center of each crepe, spreading mixture out to within 2 inches of edge. Fold sides of crepes over plum mixture, then roll very loosely. Repeat until all crepes and plum mixture have been used.

4. Serve crepes warm, each topped with a teaspoon of sour cream.

MAKES 8 CREPES
APPROXIMATELY 33 MILLIGRAMS SODIUM PER CREPE

♦ ♦ ♦ ♦ ♦

CHEESE CREPES
WITH FRESH BLUEBERRY SAUCE

▶ ▶

Some of our domestic cheeses, like ricotta and cottage cheese, have their counterparts in the fresh country cheeses of other nations, and like them are used in a variety of dishes from the sublimely sinful glories of rich cheesecakes to the elegant simplicity of the crepes included here. A wonderfully light dessert, these crepes also make a flamboyant breakfast or brunch dish.

If you cannot find dry curd cottage cheese, substitute the driest creamed cottage cheese available, but choose a no-salt-added variety. (The sodium content of creamed cottage cheese can run as high as 1,000 milligrams per cup!)

1	recipe Basic Dessert Crepes (page 191)
³/₄	cup dry curd cottage cheese
¹/₂	cup low fat ricotta cheese
2	tablespoons sugar
	Thawed frozen egg substitute equal to 1 egg
¹/₂	teaspoon vanilla extract
	Vegetable oil cooking spray

BLUEBERRY SAUCE
2	cups fresh blueberries
2	tablespoons sugar
1	tablespoon fresh lemon juice
1	teaspoon cornstarch

1. Prepare 8 large crepes in a 10- to 12-inch skillet, lightly browning them on one side only. Remove from heat and place on a flat surface, browned side facing up.

2. Combine cheeses with sugar, egg substitute, and vanilla and mix until thoroughly blended. Place about 1½ tablespoons of cheese mixture in center of each crepe. Fold over sides and roll so that cheese mixture is securely sealed inside crepe. (At this point crepes can be refrigerated or frozen for later use.)

3. To prepare sauce, combine blueberries, sugar, and lemon juice in a saucepan and cook over low heat, stirring and lightly mashing blueberries, until mixture simmers. (Add a tablespoon of water if berries are not juicy enough.) Stir in cornstarch, cover, and simmer gently, stirring occasionally, over very low heat for about 5 minutes.

4. While sauce cooks, coat a large nonstick skillet with cooking spray and heat. Add crepes to skillet and brown lightly on both sides over low heat.

5. Serve crepes hot, topped with blueberry sauce.

MAKES 8 CREPES

APPROXIMATELY 60 MILLIGRAMS SODIUM PER CREPE WITH SAUCE

♦ ♦ ♦ ♦ ♦

HOT PEAR CREPES
WITH RED CURRANT GLAZE

▶ ▶

You may substitute apples for the pears in this recipe, or try fresh, ripe peaches with apricot preserves. The point is: once you've mastered the technique for making the basic crepes, go ahead and improvise! But remember to check the sodium content of those substitutes—or any ingredient—first.

1   recipe Basic Dessert Crepes (page 191)
1   tablespoon unsalted butter or margarine, or blend
2   just-ripe pears, preferably Bartlett, peeled, halved, cored, and thinly sliced
2   tablespoons sugar
1   teaspoon fresh lemon juice
1   teaspoon cornstarch
¼   cup red currant jelly

1. Prepare crepes according to the recipe and set aside.
2. Preheat oven to 400°F.
3. Melt butter or margarine in a saucepan. Add pears, sugar, and lemon juice. Stir over low heat until mixture simmers. Stir in cornstarch. Cover, reduce heat to very low, and simmer, stirring occasionally, for 10 minutes or until pears are tender. Remove from heat and let cool slightly.
4. Spoon a small amount of pear mixture in the center of each crepe, spreading mixture out to within 2 inches of

crepe edges. Fold sides of crepes over pear mixture, then roll loosely.

5. Place filled crepes, folded side down, on a lightly greased or nonstick baking pan, and brush the surface of each crepe with a teaspoon of red currant jelly.

6. Bake for 5 to 8 minutes or until jelly melts and crepes are heated through.

MAKES 12 CREPES
APPROXIMATELY 23 MILLIGRAMS SODIUM PER CREPE

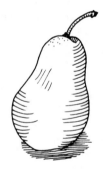

◆ ◆ ◆ ◆ ◆

PEACH AND CRANBERRY CRISP

▶ ▶

This is the kind of dessert whose divine aroma will bring the neighbors to your door, asking for a taste.

4	*ripe peaches*
2	*tablespoons fresh lemon juice*
1¹/₂	*cups fresh cranberries, picked over and rinsed*
²/₃	*cup all-purpose flour*
¹/₃	*cup firmly packed brown sugar*
3	*tablespoons unsalted butter or margarine, or blend, chilled*

1. Preheat oven to 375°F.

2. Blanch peaches in boiling water for 1 minute, plunge quickly into cold water, then peel. Halve, pit, and thinly slice peaches. Arrange slices to cover the bottom of a lightly greased casserole or nonstick baking dish (about 9 inches in diameter). Sprinkle lemon juice and cranberries over peaches.

3. Combine flour with sugar and, using a pastry blender or 2 knives, cut butter or margarine into flour and sugar until mixture is crumbly. Sprinkle over fruit.

4. Bake for about 30 minutes or until fruit is tender and coating is crisp and lightly browned.

SERVES 4

APPROXIMATELY 3 MILLIGRAMS SODIUM PER SERVING

BAKED APPLE CAKE

▶ ▶

A batter-taster's delight—but save some to bake! Fragrant and delicious, it's best served warm.

1	teaspoon plus 1 tablespoon unsalted butter/margarine blend
$1/3$	cup plain or honey-toasted wheat germ
	Thawed frozen egg substitute equal to 2 eggs
$1/4$	cup sugar
$1/4$	cup plus 2 tablespoons low sodium, low fat (2%) buttermilk
$1/4$	cup light brown sugar
3	tablespoons thawed frozen apple juice concentrate
1	cup unbleached all-purpose flour
$2/3$	cup whole wheat pastry flour
4	large tart apples, peeled, halved, cored, thinly sliced, and tossed with fresh lemon juice
1	tablespoon confectioners' sugar (optional)

1. Preheat oven to 350°F. Grease a 9-inch round or square cake pan with 1 teaspoon butter/margarine blend and sprinkle with wheat germ, pressing crumbs lightly into butter. Shake out any excess (there should not be much).

2. Beat together egg substitute and sugar until pale and lemon-colored. Add buttermilk, brown sugar, and apple juice. Beat well.

3. Sift flours over egg and milk mixture and stir until blended. Stir in apples and any accumulated juices and spoon

into prepared pan (batter should be thick). Dot top of batter with remaining tablespoon of butter/margarine blend.

4. Bake in the center of preheated oven for about 45 minutes or until cooked through and lightly browned. Remove from oven and cool for 10 minutes on a rack. Serve warm from pan sprinkled with confectioners' sugar, or cool completely.

SERVES 8
APPROXIMATELY 32 MILLIGRAMS SODIUM PER SERVING

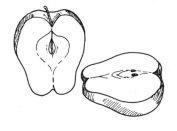

♦ ♦ ♦ ♦ ♦

SPICED ORANGE NUT CAKE

▶ ▶

This aromatic and delicious cake, cut into squares, makes a great finger food as the finale for a casual meal or as part of afternoon tea.

	Vegetable oil cooking spray
1¹/₂	cups unbleached all-purpose flour
³/₄	teaspoon baking powder
1	teaspoon ground cinnamon
¹/₄	teaspoon ground ginger
¹/₂	teaspoon ground nutmeg
	Pinch ground cloves
3	tablespoons softened unsalted butter or margarine, or blend
¹/₂	cup sugar
¹/₄	cup light brown sugar
	Thawed frozen egg substitute equal to 2 eggs
¹/₃	cup low fat (2%) milk
1	teaspoon vanilla extract
2	tablespoons orange zest (from approximately 1 large orange)
¹/₄	cup orange juice, preferably not fresh-squeezed
¹/₄	teaspoon anise seeds
¹/₄	cup chopped walnuts
1	tablespoon confectioners' sugar (optional)

1. Preheat oven to 350°F. Cut a square of waxed paper to fit the bottom of an 8-inch-square baking pan and lightly coat with cooking spray.

2. In a small bowl, sift together flour, baking powder, cinnamon, ginger, nutmeg, and cloves and set aside.

3. In a large bowl, combine butter or margarine and sugars and beat until creamy. Add egg substitute and beat well.

4. Add milk and flour mixture alternately to egg mixture in about 4 additions, combining well after each addition. Mix in vanilla, orange zest and juice, anise, and walnuts.

5. Transfer batter to prepared pan and bake in center of oven for 45 minutes or until top is springy to the touch. Remove from oven, cool on rack for 5 minutes, then invert and peel off waxed paper. Cool completely. Dust lightly with confectioners' sugar before serving, if desired.

MAKES SIXTEEN 2-INCH SQUARES
APPROXIMATELY 30 MILLIGRAMS SODIUM PER SQUARE

◆ ◆ ◆ ◆ ◆

WHITE ANGEL FOOD CAKE WITH HOT CHOCOLATE SAUCE

▶ ▶

Some prefer their angel food cake straight—that is, un-adorned by sauce. I offer the sauce in a sauce boat and let folks choose for themselves. Incidentally, the cake is delicious toasted the next day.

1¹/₂	cups cake flour, sifted
¹/₂	cup plus ¹/₃ cup sugar, divided and sifted
12	large egg whites, at room temperature
1	teaspoon cream of tartar
1¹/₂	teaspoons vanilla extract
1¹/₂	teaspoons fresh lemon juice

CHOCOLATE SAUCE

3	tablespoons sugar
³/₄	cup evaporated skim milk
1	teaspoon vanilla extract
1	tablespoon cocoa powder
¹/₂	tablespoon cornstarch
2	teaspoons unsalted butter or margarine, or blend

1. Preheat oven to 350°F. Set aside a scrupulously clean, ungreased 10-inch tube pan with removable bottom.

2. In a small bowl, resift flour and ¹/₂ cup sugar together.

3. In a large, grease-free, nonplastic bowl, whip egg whites until frothy. Sprinkle in cream of tartar and beat whites until soft peaks form. Gradually add remaining ¹/₃ cup sugar, beating until stiff peaks form.

4. Resift flour and sugar mixture over egg whites, folding gently but quickly until just blended. Fold in vanilla and lemon juice.

5. Pour batter into pan and bake for 1 hour or until cake pulls away from the side of the pan and is lightly golden. Remove from oven and invert pan over the pointed end of a funnel. Cool completely before removing from pan.

6. Prepare sauce while cake bakes. Combine sugar, milk, and vanilla in a small, nonstick saucepan. Cook over very low heat, stirring, until sugar is dissolved and mixture is smooth. Whisk in cocoa powder, cornstarch, and butter. Cook over medium heat for about 3 minutes or until thickened—do not boil. (Sauce can be reheated by setting bowl in a pan of hot water.)

7. To serve, slice cake into 12 portions and top each slice with 1 tablespoon sauce.

SERVES 12
APPROXIMATELY 90 MILLIGRAMS SODIUM PER SERVING

◆◆◆◆◆

SIMPLE LEMON MOUSSE

▶▶▶▶▶▶▶▶▶▶▶▶▶▶▶▶▶▶▶▶▶▶▶▶▶

Light and lemony, the perfect finale to a fish dinner.

$^1/_3$ cup sugar
$^1/_4$ cup water
1   cup fresh lemon juice
1   envelope unflavored gelatin
1   cup evaporated skim milk (chilled in bowl in
     freezer for 1 hour; chill beaters as well)
1   teaspoon vanilla extract
     Fresh mint leaves for garnish

1. Combine sugar and water in medium saucepan, heat to boiling, and stir just until sugar is dissolved. Add ¾ cup lemon juice, stir to blend, and reduce heat.

2. In a small bowl, moisten gelatin in remaining lemon juice. Let stand 2 minutes. Add gelatin to lemon and sugar mixture, bring to a boil, and remove from heat. Let mixture cool (it should be cool but not set).

3. Remove evaporated milk from freezer (there should be a thick rim of slush around the edges) and beat with vanilla until stiff. Fold into cooled lemon mixture. Pour into a serving bowl or individual dishes or stemmed goblets and chill until completely set. Serve garnished with mint.

SERVES 4

APPROXIMATELY 81 MILLIGRAMS SODIUM PER SERVING

BRANDIED PUMPKIN PIE

Pumpkin pie is a natural for salt watchers—pumpkin is very low in sodium and the variety of spices in this pie makes the addition of salt unnecessary.

    ¹/₄   *cup rolled oats*
     1   *cup all-purpose flour*
     3   *tablespoons unsalted butter or margarine, or*
          blend
          Ice water
     1   *1-pound can pumpkin puree, drained of any*
          surface liquid
    ¹/₂   *cup sugar*
     3   *tablespoons dark brown sugar*
     1   *teaspoon vanilla extract*
    ³/₄   *teaspoon ground cinnamon*
    ¹/₄   *teaspoon ground nutmeg*
    ¹/₄   *teaspoon ground allspice*
    ¹/₂   *teaspoon ground cardamom*
     1   *cup evaporated skim milk*
          Thawed frozen egg substitute equal to 2 eggs
     2   *tablespoons unflavored brandy*
    ¹/₄   *cup coarsely ground pecans (optional)*

1. Combine oats and flour in the work bowl of a food processor and process quickly just to blend ingredients and chop up oats. Add butter or margarine and cut in just until mixture is crumbly. With machine running, add ice water,

one tablespoon at a time, just until mixture begins to form a ball (do not overblend). Remove from bowl, enclose in plastic wrap, and chill for 15 minutes.

2. Preheat oven to 350°F.

3. Roll out dough thinly and fit into an ungreased 9-inch pie plate, trimming off any excess. Prick bottom of dough in several places and bake for 10 minutes. Remove from oven and cool completely.

4. When crust is almost cool, preheat oven to 375°F.

5. Combine remaining ingredients, except pecans, in a large bowl and beat until well blended (you can use an electric mixer or food processor with a large work bowl).

6. Sprinkle the bottom surface of the crust with pecans, pour pumpkin mixture into crust, and bake for 1 hour. Cool on rack before serving.

SERVES 8

APPROXIMATELY 63 MILLIGRAMS SODIUM PER SERVING

INDEX